THE CRISIS OF RELIGIOUS LIFE

THE CRISIS OF RELIGIOUS LIFE

By Thaddee Matura

Author of *Celibacy and Community: The Gospel Foundations for Religious Life*

Translated by
PAUL SCHWARTZ and PAUL LACHANCE

FRANCISCAN HERALD PRESS
Chicago, Illinois 60609

The Crisis of Religious Life, by Thaddée Matura, translated from the original French work, *La Vie Religieuse au Tournant,* published in 1971 by Les Editions du Cerf, Paris. Copyright © 1973 by Franciscan Herald Press, 1434 West 51st Street, Chicago, Illinois 60609. Library of Congress Catalog Number: 73-4718. Cataloging in Publication Data: · BX2435.M39413 248'.894. ISBN: 0-8199-0453-8. Made in the United States of America.

~~~~~~

NIHIL OBSTAT:
　Mark Hegener O.F.M.
　Censor Deputatus

IMPRIMATUR:
　Msgr. Richard A. Rosemeyer, J.C.D.
　Vicar General, Archdiocese of Chicago

May 22, 1973

FOREWORD

Christianity once more is being brought to the test. It is passing through criticism and contradiction so vigorous that only what is strong and based on solid faith will survive. One after another, every part of the Church finds itself called into question. Religious life — which seemed to have escaped this evolution longer than, for example, the ministry — has also entered a period of crisis. A general re-thinking of the question, at once practical and theoretical, is taking place in all of its aspects. Reflection on its Biblical and human foundations, as well as an analysis of the contemporary situation is widespread, and in the last two years published works on this subject have multiplied.[1]

Having published a rather systematic study[2] on religious life not too long ago, as well as an article analyzing the current situation,[3] I intend to continue with these reflections in this book, only from a more practical angle. What will be set forth and discussed here presupposes as a point of departure the thesis set forth in *Celibacy and Community*, a thesis which has received rather favorable critical acclaim.[4] But it has appeared necessary to expand this thesis and to make distinctions in tackling the various problems, theoretical as well as practical, which grip those in religious life.

Our study begins with an analysis of the current situation in religious life, an analysis which, cursory as it is, hopes to take into account the available sociological data, statistics, and historical research, concentrating on the description of current trends which transform this life. Following this will be a reflection, no doubt theoretical, but still at the root of our effort, on the specific nature of the religious vocation in the midst of Christian life. Religious life does not simply play a role of social or ecclesiastical service, it is not a "Christianization" of certain universal human values (interior life, asceticism), or the way of greater perfection; neither is it purely and simply identical with gospel radicalism. It is an original realization of the Christian vocation lived in celibacy and community.

The chapter which follows tries to show by a detailed analysis that most of the elements considered peculiar to the religious life (primacy of the gospel, prayer, community, asceticism, poverty, chastity, obedience) are, in fact, held in common and are integral to all Christian life which takes itself seriously. Religious life holds no monopoly over this; at the very most it is an original realization of a serious Christian life. These values must be liberated and rendered open to all Christians. This in no way deprecates religious life, but proposes new challenges for every Christian life.

Another chapter touches upon a certain number of questions currently much in debate: religious celibacy, its Scriptural basis, theological and psychological meaning; lifelong commitment, its possibility and meaning in human life; historical continuity in various spiritual families; and finally, the question of religious life lived either separately or mixed with other realities.

To conclude, an essential question is raised: that of faith and prayer in religious life. In the current crisis of faith, have religious been protected from this? Does not religious life, on the contrary, require a never-ending deepening of this faith which stands, in a certain way, condemned to continuing vulnerability? Prayer appears as a privileged and necessary expression of this faith. In this lies its importance, as well as the necessity of reflection on the forms which need to be adopted in the unprecedented situations in which prayer is offered today.

In proposing these reflections, some of which diverge from generally accepted positions, especially chapters II and III, I in no way pretend to bring definitive answers to a problem as complex and far-reaching as the meaning of religious life. If this book can shed some light, no matter how faint, on what is being sought after and is so important for the future of this life, then our purpose will have been achieved. For this book has no other purpose than to serve the thought and research of so many brothers and sisters throughout the world who seek to live the gospel of Jesus Christ in the common life and celibacy, and thanks to whom this has been written.

CONTENTS

By Thaddee Matura

Author of Celibacy and Community: The Gospel Foundations for Religious Life

Translated by
PAUL SCHWARTZ and PAUL LACHANCE

FRANCISCAN HERALD PRESS
Chicago, Illinois 60609

Chapter I

RELIGIOUS LIFE TODAY

Even if religious life in the past might have appeared to be a world apart from, or at least marginal to, the real world of men and women, it is today less and less so. For it participates, for better or worse, in the evolution and general re-thinking of everything happening at all levels of society and the Church. It is not possible, then, to describe religious life in the world of today without situating it within the wake of diverse currents sweeping across and penetrating areas heretofore reserved to the Church.

To speak of currents and their orientations obliges us to enter into a dynamic and evolutionary way of thinking: one speaks of something which is already undergoing change. Even that religious life which certain people wished to see as the symbol of what is steady and unchangeable, experiences accelerated change today. This must be kept in mind during the course of this chapter where an attempt is made to sketch a sort of typology of contemporary religious life, after a quick indication has first been given of the major axes around which the world and the Church revolve; for, without this it would be truly difficult to understand what is going on.

I. TECHNOLOGICAL AND CULTURAL CHANGE IN THE WORLD

It is foolhardy indeed to try to describe in a few paragraphs the major characteristics shaping the world in which we live, and there is a risk in contenting oneself with the slogans repeated

3

everywhere. One must nevertheless try to bring out the major trends of the evolution in which we find ourselves involved. For if a lot of myth and faddishness already exist around such words as: technological society, consumer society, secularization, desacralization, etc., — words of which one must know enough to be critical — it is no less true that the realities designated by these words make up the world in which we live and breathe.

So, it is beyond question that we are witnesses to profound changes at the heart of western society, which is, with some important exceptions, in fact global society. We live the phenomena of urbanization at an accelerated rhythm with the establishment of great metropolises where men and women are crowded together in a certain anonymity. Work itself is undergoing change through automation and the use of computers. The standard of living is rising steadily, at least in the northern hemisphere, dragging all men with it in the cycle of production and consumption. The mass media extend their networks everywhere: through the press, radio, and television, the speed of travel and of communication everyone can live and be informed at the same time, so that the world of today appears at this level as a global village (McLuhan).

Unity and, certainly, standardization are the results of this evolution, at least for the western world. But at the same time a social disparity deepens in an increasingly scandalous way; sometimes within capitalist societies themselves, but constantly so between the populations of the northern hemisphere and those of the Third World (Asia, Africa, Latin America). This objective injustice, which no one seems able to prevent and which instead grows more serious (would revolution be necessary to reverse the trend?), could very well be the foremost problem of the coming years.

Against this technological background a cultural evolution, one of mentalities, is taking place as well. While the question is one of facts, we are actually in the presence of spiritual currents, more difficult to grasp and describe objectively. What characterizes this mentality is first of all a rejection of the static. There is a marked preference for mobility, for what moves and evolves; concepts of essence or nature are unpopular. The absolute, the objective, seems to have less value than the relative in the process of realization. Ethical norms are no longer bound to a few unchangeable principles, but are invented from direct contact with the concrete situation. A pre-established hierarchical order is rejected along with the concept of authority linked to it; one finds in contemporary civilization the rejection, if not the death, of the Father. For one concerned with life in society, the democratic view necessitates participation, co-responsibility, and the greatest possible measure of personal freedom; at the heart of cities which depersonalize and crowd men together, an individualist current is nevertheless strong.

Concerning the religious dimension of man, it is easy to get lost in the forest of varied opinions which exist on this topic. For while it may be true that the scientific, positivist formation of most men and women eliminates the religious attitudes which are regarded as "magical," "superstitious," or "compensating," it is not at all certain that these do not find refuge or transference elsewhere (for example, astrology, horoscopes, etc). Has secularization only brought out the distinction between the human reality in its autonomy and the depth or religious dimension of man, or has it completely eliminated all reference other than man reduced to his biological and psychic make-up? Is the "sacred" a residue of a pre-logical and mythical mentality, or is it a fundamental dimension of existence? Reading the abundant literature on these questions, one is led to say that man and woman who have come of age live in a secularized world without any reference whatever to something beyond or to some transcendence, — in a technical and rational world where he or she is left with his or her own freedom or initiative.

But is this trend in the process of being reversed? Isn't the reaction of young people today — to mention only the hippie phenomenon — a reaction which challenges, ultimately, all the characteristics of technological society, which calls for the reign of imagination, and which invites everyone to perpetual celebration, utopian as it might seem — is it not a protest against the impersonal, rationalistic, and shortsighted view of the present day? Are these young people merely unadapted marginals who respond as unconscious reactionaries against a world which scares them? Are they not rather, foretelling, even beckoning, the advent of a world other than ours where men and women will finally live all their dimensions?

Thus, when giving an outline portraying a certain image of the world in process, one needs to beware of hardening its characteristics. For, this world is not so rigid that one cannot bend and influence its evolution; in this aspect it resembles the men and women who make it. To situate oneself as a Christian or religious in such a world does not mean blind adherence to any particular current as it manifests itself, but discernment in the midst of a mobile (or moving) situation of where the future lies, and of commitment to that future by concrete action.

II. EVOLUTION IN THE CHURCH

The Church, "creation of the Word," while different and distinct from the world as seen in its concrete reality, is for this reason no less totally immersed in it than the leaven in the dough. The people who shape it, the sociological form of its institutions, the currents of thought which animate it — in short, the totality of its life stands in strict dependence on the present situation of the world. It participates with all its being in all the change affecting humanity which is called to be its body. If the Church, especially in its "Roman" form, appeared until about 1960 as a haven of order and calm (not to say immobility) in the midst of a world in upheaval, such is no longer the case today. In contrast to what it was before, the Church now seems to be swept away by the storm like a rudderless ship. This is especially so on the level of its structures and theological opinion.

The precision, the multiplicity, and often, the rigidity of the

Church structures are well known. Canon law, the rules, and the constitutions, not to mention the liturgical rubrics, all determined in a detailed way "right conduct" in general and specific circumstances for the entire Church and for particular groups such as religious. Almost everything was well-defined, foreseen, and catalogued. The reflections of moralists went even further by fixing obligations and responsibilities. If Christian freedom was not always well-respected, responsibility not recognized, nor the danger of legalism avoided within this well-delimited space, there was at least the security of precise norms. To be sure, many Christians had trouble breathing in this setting; others left for less protected fields.

In these last few years, however, the fortified edifice of ecclesiastical structures seems to have been torn down stone by stone. The rigidity of the past is loosening everywhere; frameworks collapse; all becomes flexible, to the point that most of the time, Christians, whether lay, religious, or cleric, are left to the choice of their own initiatives. No longer does an impersonal law trace the line of conduct, but it is done by the judgment of believers conscious of having to respond to God and to the community of their brothers and sisters. Freedom and responsibility, freedom and authority: one sees that the new situation is no less demanding than the other. Different as it may be, its requirements are greater and more difficult. For, as the exterior law loses its importance and the framework which it set crumbles, the necessity of searching, of being confronted with the word of God and with those responsible for proclaiming it will demand much maturity and a great loyalty.

Not only is the legal framework evolving, but something deeper and more delicate is happening. The expressions of Christian faith, its content and interpretation are also subject to alteration; a cause of rejoicing for some, uneasiness for others.

There has always been a certain flexibility, a certain relativism, in this area, but this was known and practiced mostly by theologians and historians. The average Christian learned formulas and received explanations which may have been intended to be adaptable and contemporary, but which imposed themselves with authority. Without exaggerating unduly, it can be said that a kind of dogmatism held sway and most people accommodated themselves quite well. The only thing necessary was intervention of the Holy Office, or the pope himself, for a doctrinal question to be considered definitively settled, or at least withdrawn from free discussion.

We are far from these times today. The faith of the Church is an object of doubt and contestation. There is obviously nothing extraordinary in research, hypotheses, or attempts at new explanations, since Christian thinkers in all times have scrutinized the faith entrusted to the Church. However, it is something relatively new, in the modern era at any rate, for the fundamentals to be placed in question, discussed, and occasionally rejected; and this, so to speak, on the public platform of the Church. While such attitudes are usually countered by pastors, the fact is that a certain flexibility or even imprecision prevails in the domain of faith (its expression and content), and many live in uncertainty. One can, and must in certain cases, deplore this situation, but it does not help to close one's eyes to this relativism and these doubts.

All the more so, since they in fact touch the very center of the faith. It would be truly superficial to believe that the re-thinking which we have mentioned reaches only the periphery of the faith: such items as the ministry of priests (its status), the sociological structures of the Church, liturgical expressions, or some of the language of faith. Even the problem of the Church as an institution — something already more fundamental — and its relationship to the world is not at the heart of this debate. What is in question today is the reality of God and Christ. The faith of the Christian is being challenged on this ultimate point. Who is God? Is he a reality other than the human? Is Jesus the human *par excellence* by his complete self-transcendence, but nothing more? Is the Resurrection simply an affirmation of his ever-present influence, or is it a real victory over death, both his and ours? Indeed, this is the point to which our discussion comes when we push the questions as far as they will go.

The theological turmoil of the last forty years linked to the names of Barth, Bultmann, Bonhoeffer, Tillich, and Rahner has ended up reaching the masses of Christians through a simplified popularization. This has, of course, afforded it a large audience, but it has also warped the data of the problem. Most persons, even among those who have studied theology, are ignorant of the complex ideas and thought nuances of these authors, except through Robinson's writings in *Honest to God,* or some article in *Time* or *Newsweek* on the "death of God." But here again it is essential to hold fast to the facts as they are.

What is at stake here is the very basis of the Christian being which, no doubt, often gives rise to another question: What is the specific nature of the Christian faith? In what does the Christian distinguish himself from any other man or woman open to something beyond? Does the Christian have a word to say, a message? What is this word; what does it have that is new? The problem, so often discussed, of the relationship of the Church to the world is without doubt linked to this search for identity. If the Church must be the leaven and the driving force of humanity, if it must serve a critical function, it can do so only from a clear awareness of its own particular being. Now, at the same time as we find doubt about God and Christ, we discover uncertainty everywhere about one's self, about the meaning of just who one is. This is true for Christians in general, as well as for the different vocations and ministries in the community.

This enumeration or description of the major orientations influencing the evolution of humanity and the Church, cursory and superficial though it is, at least allows us to situate and understand better the present reality of religious life. Since this is being lived by men and women of our own time, one must expect to meet at its heart the same tendencies and the same problems.

III. THE SITUATION OF RELIGIOUS LIFE

1. Statistics.

One must begin by presenting certain statistics which allow us to make useful comparisons and initiate reflections. Since we lack data from the Eastern Church where religious life — more or less flourishing, depending on the country — exists and develops, and setting aside all Anglican and other Protestant religious, whose number is not large, we will be concerned here only with religious life in the Catholic Church. We understand religious life as defined in present law: an approved form of life where one publicly commits himself or herself to living in celibacy, poverty, and obedience.

The round figures which are given vary between 331,000 and 276,000 for religious men and 886,000 and 1,081,000 for religious women,[5] which gives us a total of about 1,300,000. This number appears quite large if we compare this group with that of the diocesan clergy (about 300,000), but it hardly represents more than 0.20% of the total number of Catholics in the world (more than 500 million). Furthermore, the number is decreasing considerably in general; the precise statistics available, which are rare, indicate this trend. Thus the Order of Friars Minor decreased by 1,487 between 1963 (27,140 members) and 1968 (25,653), a decrease of more than 5% in five years.[6] The Jesuits, 36,038 in 1965, were only 33,828 in 1970, a decrease of 2,210 in five years — more than 6%.[7] As far as religious women are concerned, in France there has been a decrease of about 13% since 1945.[8] This reduction is due, certainly, to deaths among members, but also to the more and more numerous departures and the constant decrease of entrants. (Thus, in the Order of Friars Minor there were 952 entering the novitiate in 1963, but only 674 in 1968, or 278 fewer, a decrease of about 30%.)[9] Obviously, these facts would have to be established exactly in order to interpret them properly.

If one tries to produce a historical chart of religious life, one must begin with the forms which go back to the fifth and sixth centuries; one is concerned here with the monastic life described in the rule of Benedict. On the male side, there are the Benedictine monks and the Cistercian reform, plus related groups, few in number, totaling about 20,000 (7% of all religious). The women monastic groups of the same tradition number 14,000 (a little more than 1% of women religious).[10] One moves on from this to groups of medieval origin, almost exclusively thirteenth century. Among men, this group, with 75,000 members, makes up 25% of the total. The Franciscan family is the most numerous (47,000 or 70% of the group), followed by the Dominicans (10,000), Carmelites (7,000), and other communities whose total strength is less. The women religious of the same origins are about 36,000 (18,000 in the Franciscan family; 12,000 Carmelites; 6,000 Dominicans); that is to say, more than 3% of the total.

Communities born in the sixteenth century have about 42,000 members (14%), of which total the Jesuits alone (35,000) represent nearly 90%. About 30,000 religious (10%) have their origin in the eighteenth century (Christian Brothers, 17,000; Redemptorists, 9,000); the Sisters of Charity, most numerous among the women religious (45,000), is the only women's group going back to this period. In fact, women's religious life in its modern form, without cloister, found its growth especially in the nineteenth century.

The nineteenth century is fecund in religious creativity. About 42% of religious men and almost the total number of religious women derive their origin from this period. Except for the Salesians, who exceed 22,000, we find numerous groups (hundreds on the women's side) whose total strength rarely exceeds a thousand members.

This interest in numbers and classifications is not to indicate the influence of any particular group, but only to show the historical permanence of these movements, often very old, as well as their orientation. Schematically, one could say that religious life in the West has known four births: fifth and sixth centuries: monasticism; thirteenth century: gospel movements; sixteenth century: gospel and struggle of the Faith; eighteenth and nineteenth centuries: service of the Church and the world.

In our day new forms have appeared, initiating deep transformations. There are, for instance, the secular institutes, whose numbers and strength are not well known (except for Opus Dei, which has some 50,000 members), but whose impact on the evolution of religious life is very great. Without going into the always unresolved discussion of their status (are they religious or lay?), let us say that the secular character of their work and their presence, their rejection of artificial separation and signs which express such an attitude, has opened the way to important transformations among the religious themselves. They are distinguished from the latter, if not at least by their anonymity, usually by the secrecy of their commitment and often by the absence of community life. But aside from these points — important to be sure — one sees less and less how their commitment and their style of life differs from that of so many religious today.[11]

In fact, new forms of religious life have emerged since 1945: the spiritual family of Charles de Foucauld (Little Brothers and Sisters of Jesus) and the Community of Taize. Of little importance numerically if one compares them with the older orders, these two groups have played a considerable role, far beyond their numbers. At the same time that they maintain their community life, publicly manifesting their status as religious, they have initiated a new style of life which revives the fresh forms of the beginnings, often reaching back centuries — whether to the sixth or the thirteenth. What distinguishes them from religious life in its classical form is that they have taken, in their home life and in their work, a contemporary type of living: life in small groups; the non-ownership of institutional buildings and the renting of apartments; the adoption of a professional life which is outside the fraternity or community, and which is not, of itself, at the service of the community or the Church.

Moreover, these two movements are solidly rooted in values considered basic: a gospel evangelism, intense prayer life, emphasis on the fraternity itself, and presence to the world. These have played a role of stimulus and example for the efforts of renewal undertaken among the religious of more ancient traditions. Again, as so many times in history, the charism of some has contributed to the awakening and edification of all.

2. Present Evolution.

As we have just seen, the entirety of religious life, whether masculine or feminine, is attached to the more or less remote past. Today it is shaken by currents which push it toward transformations which often appear radical. This is not to say that the old orders have not been submitted to evolutions in the past which, without being quite spectacular, have nonetheless had some effect on their image — not to mention desired "reforms" which most of them have experienced. One need only think of the various mendicant orders of today: the three Franciscan branches (there were once at least ten), and the Augustinian and Carmelite reforms. What is happening today is without a doubt a part of the usual historical process of transformation and adaptation which reaches all living bodies.

The present evolution within the ancient groups appears to us to be oriented in two directions: the increasing flexibility and modernization of the existing structures, and the search for new forms. The first is the work of the general chapters; the second comes from grassroot initiatives.

(a) General chapters.

General chapters of "aggiornamento" are the fruit of the Council and the application of its decrees. Prescribed by the Council, they were the official expression, in most religious families, of a movement of theoretical and practical research undertaken almost universally.[12]

The work of these chapters resulted above all in a return to sources; Gospel sources first of all, since for all religious the Gospel remains the supreme rule and calling. That we still fall short of this work is evident. The Gospel is never definitively understood, neither in its universal message, nor as a basis for a certain type of Christian life which religious strive to realize. Even further, the question of the Gospel basis of religious life is hardly raised at all, and the field remains wide open for the exploration of exegetes and spiritual men and women.

The proper source for each religious family is the charism of its origins; the experience of its founder and his first companions, the project which they elaborated, lived, and expressed by a rule of life, according to their setting and time. Here again, the attempt has been made to know in a more completely historical fashion the intuitions and realizations of the origins in order to interpret and apply them to situations today. This second renewal derived from the sources is not as simple as one might believe at first glance. While some families are linked to strong and radiant personalities and their vital influence, as attested by numerous documents and rich tradition, others have trouble finding in their beginnings an originality which holds meaning for today. The more the origins are linked to a need determined by a period, the more the transposition appears difficult. At any rate, this plunge into history may delineate certain lines capable of inspiring current conduct, and will likewise encourage a healthy self-criticism in comparison with the original dynamism; for certain families, on the other hand, it raises the survival question and their *raison d'etre* in the world of today.

An important task has been accomplished by the chapters in the transformation of the internal structures of religious life. The basic notion of the community as a milieu for fraternal life — privileged space where mutual love is lived — has been strongly put into evidence. Moving out of this theme of community or fraternity, we have tried to rethink and resituate the relationships between authority and freedom. Even where one has sought to maintain the paternal image for authority (monastic tradition), the emphasis lies on the notion of the service that one exercises, the participation of everyone in the responsibility, as well as the respect and the autonomy due to every person. Even if this new orientation is not always followed in practice, the concept of obedience has unquestionably evolved considerably. Generally speaking, the same is true for the concrete organization of life. Conceived in a detailed and rigid fashion in the past (minute prescriptions on the subject of daily life, schedules, relationships, etc.), now a new flexibility has been rediscovered; only major orientations are suggested; the concrete decisions of each will determine the details. This holds as well for the important area of the formation of candidates. In the face of the prevailing uncertainty in this matter, a few directions have been indicated, leaving practical application for local decision.

As for the insertion of religious life into the world — its presence — this step is without question more timid. All are aware of their link with men and women — whether believers or not — and of the necessity of living for them and with them. Thus a certain flexibility has been introduced, even in the orders traditionally cut off from the world, regarding "separation," which was often artificial. The desire for hospitality, for the reception of others, and for a prayer both open and accessible to all has been affirmed. But a problem remains: that of the professional life of the religious, or, if one prefers, their work.

Until now this work has been exercised almost exclusively within the religious structure or for its profit. For the men, those who were priests — and this is the case for more than two-thirds[13] devoted themselves to different forms of the priestly ministry, unless they found themselves teaching or in religious or ecclesiastical administration. The others were responsible for the apostolate identified with their institute, especially in teaching, or in menial labor, since most houses attempted to be self-sufficient.

For the women — except those monastics living self-sufficiently or off the gifts of the faithful — this meant responsibility for educational, medical, or charitable institutions, dependent mostly on the congregations. This situation lent itself to the image that the religious world was tightly linked to the services and institutions of the Church. There is, surely, nothing to be criticized in this view when one admits the necessity — or at least the provisional utility — of such institutions. But the question arises whether the religious life is destined to be at the service of the stewardship of the Church for the purpose of creating and maintaining services more or less in competition with those of society (education, health services, etc.).

Thus a certain number of groups have foreseen the possibility of their members taking up professional or manual work in societal ventures. This is obviously an altogether revolutionary opening (though the secular institutes and the Little Brothers of Jesus have taken to this road for quite some time now), especially if this orientation should prevail over the traditional model.

These are, it seems to me, the striking characteristics of the searchings undertaken by the general chapters. They have not sought to replace one structure with another of the same type, even with an "improved" version, but rather to allow for greater flexibility, for mobility, for open doors. All the more so, since the notion and meaning of law are in evolution and one must consider the new mentality.

(b) *Grassroot initiatives.*

The new orientations proposed by these chapters have brought about important transformations within these communities. Many elements have been changed: the dress code, the style of fraternal relationship, the relationship between superior and subject, the way of prayer, of work, etc. And the evolution continues apace. But those who think that one must go even further are numerous. The style of life (large groups, special houses), the style of insertion and the type of activity which still remains tributary to a certain conception linked to the past, appear to them needful of more radical modification.

Moreover, beginning with the premises which the official orientations already contained in germ, many groups are committing themselves to avenues yet little explored. These "fraternities" or "new communities," as they are called, grow a little everywhere today, like mushrooms, in Europe and North America. Their number is not fully known, but they are in the hundreds. They are mostly male groups, but religious women are also involved. Most of the orders are implicated, preponderantly those of medieval or monastic origin. These experiences continue with the approbation and support of those responsible, or at least with their tolerance. Some have existed for ten years now, but most date from two to three years back at the most. Without affirming that the road they take is the only one open in the future, one can state that there exists here an original effort at the expression of the permanent reality of the religious life in the world of today. We shall try to describe some of the characteristics of this new phenomenon.

We are almost always concerned here with small groups of four or five members. The choice of such a figure is dictated by psychological reasons: it is believed that this is an optimal number favoring true human relations. There are also socio-economic factors: such a group inserts itself easily in the normal setting of life and work; it appears as a family and not as an institution.

The fundamental value that this group proposes to live is the fraternity, deepened from within and open to all relationships of the outside. This fraternity is not lived in the perspective of direct apostolate, but as a gratuitous sign of human and gospel friendship. Many think that such a sign, rooted as it is in the Christian life of faith and love, furnishes of itself sufficient justification for religious life.

Often, in fact, one does not attempt to underline other aspects. On the contrary, in what concerns everyday life, the profession, one desires to be like all other men and women, living a secular life. From this follows the choice of housing (often a rental in a building), salaried work, contacts, and a general style of life. Certainly, the difference will be shown in the commitment always renewed in faith, with its demands (prayer), as well as the fraternal life made possible thanks to celibacy. But the totality of the barriers which heretofore served as marks of distinction no longer exist.

Let us add that until now the insertion has taken place mostly in urban settings, although here and there tendencies are manifested to seek a country life or solitude.

All of this raises questions which we will need to discuss further, but the fact remains that there is a current which evokes what is youthful, and which could prove a turning point for religious life. If one reflects on the forms being elaborated, do we not stand awaiting a gestation which has not manifested itself for many centuries? If one considers religious life as it has been lived since the Middle Ages, one gains the impression that it has not basically changed very much at all. A religious of 1930 or even 1950 would find himself or herself more at home, perhaps, in a community of the seventeenth century than in a small city fraternity in 1970. We understand, then, why so many are asking themselves where religious life is going. Is it towards disintegration and disappearance, or, rather, towards a new and wonderful effervescence?

As we have just seen, the newness of the current described above consists essentially in a particular type of insertion into the life of men and women. So that, at least since the high Middle Ages — with the exception of the brief episode of the Franciscan beginnings — religious life has unfolded itself in a different material framework, separated (special houses, dress, sacralized domestic life, etc.), and either in the exercise of a sacerdotal ministry or at the service of a Church apostolate. Today there is a desire that at the level of domestic life and profession, this life is to be no different from the life of the common man or woman. This modification evolves, no doubt, from the new structures of society: the religious can no longer live according to a system which is tied to an outdated social regime (rural exploitation for the abbeys, gifts from the faithful, and the religious "honorarium"). How can it affirm and manifest, from this insertion, the sign peculiar to religious life?

Such a question raises many others: What is the specific nature of this life and its relationship to Christian life, of which it is but another form? What are the problems which it confronts today, especially its link to faith?

The chapters which follow will try to suggest possible answers, along the lines we have discussed. They will have in mind the totality of religious life today, but especially the new tendencies which are taking shape. These tendencies, as we have just seen, undergo the test of life while seeking a practical realization which appears to some to be risky, if not destructive of tradition.

For others, fewer in number, no doubt, they already seem to be outdated and outpaced by the evolution which runs farther and faster in its radicalism. Without pretending to give *the* answer or infallible guidelines, I will try to offer reflections based on theological, historical and spiritual data, and also on experience.

Chapter II

SPECIFIC NATURE OF THE RELIGIOUS LIFE

The psychological theme of the search for identity concerns not only individuals, but groups as well. In both cases, one must be — or rather, become — oneself, affirming one's own uniqueness, according to those traits which confer a specific character; that is, those traits which differentiate one from another. To be oneself is identity; not to be another is to distinguish oneself by a specific mark.

We know the constitutive importance of this process in the life of man and woman. More aware and more intense at certain moments of existence (for example, during adolescence, at the change of life, in situations where man or woman is threatened in his or her uniqueness), it is always a permanent dynamism around which the personality is built. The loss of personality is a serious psychic disorder; its constant search, on the other hand, reveals the progressive and unending character of personalization. When the search for identity becomes foremost, however, turning to obsession, it is often symptomatic of a crisis. The person finds himself uncertain about his selfhood; he no longer knows who he is or where he is going, and feels threatened by disintegration.

What is lived in such a way at the level of the person is operative also among human groups integrated in a certain structure of unity: national, religious, or cultural. These groups feel united as communities by values, references, and structures which confer a sort of identity upon them, encircling and uniting them as persons. They usually live in the tranquil possession of this unity, taking it very much for granted, although much effort is expended in order to maintain, or if need be, to revive it through intellectual, symbolic, or ritual means. The global milieu need only evolve and change, provoking radical questioning or confrontation, and the group undergoes an identity crisis.

It is almost a banality to assert this as a fact for all groups today. The rapid change of the world, the confrontation and often the disintegration of its structures, and the absence of new models which can assert themselves force men and women to define themselves in relationship to unprecedented situations in a way which safeguards the uniqueness proper to each group while adapting it to change. This does not happen without difficulty, nor without very serious, if occasional, tensions and even ruptures. For, one must discover the difficult road between the hardening of opposition and a surrender to the fluctuations of the moment.

The search for identity in religious life is situated at these crossroads. Like the Church from which it is inseparable, religious life today is being challenged, contested, and rejected; and not only by those on the outside. If it is true that not long ago this life appeared to be sure of itself and sheltered from basic questioning, such is no longer the case. One can find this deplorable, and think that it would be preferable to live simply without discussion or theorizing; but one cannot disclaim the facts which exist. These offer no doubt that religious life is in crisis — to search for one's identity shows that one does not perceive it clearly, that it is in doubt and escapes us — but there are also positive aspects. The turning point confronting religious life today can provide an extraordinary opportunity to dispose of what is antiquated, without life or significance, and to recover a new dynamism to which the new conditions call us.

Since, today, the concern of committed religious and of Christians wishing to live according to a common vocation is to glimpse at least the main axis around which the religious life of the future will be built, it is important to reflect on the specific nature of this life from the viewpoint of today's perspective. In this chapter we will examine and discuss the various points of view of this problem.

The question raised is at once simple and fundamental. It is a question of knowing the place and meaning of religious life in relationship to the Christian vocation as proposed by the Word of God revealed in Jesus Christ. The religious life is (or at least desires to be) Christian life; this is obvious, and yet in the midst of this general and unique vocation, it is also — and this is a concrete historical fact — something original, different, and specific. We must search for that in which this specific nature resides.

Let us hasten to add, in order to avoid all confusion from the outset, that this specific nature, important as it is in defining and distinguishing, can have no more than a secondary importance in relationship to the type which it determines. Clearly, the primary importance is to be a Christian and to be so without reservation. That one lives the call of the Gospel in a particular situation (as a lay person, religious, or as one responsible for a ministry) is in itself an accidental determination. But when one seeks to describe the identity and the specific nature of the religious as such, for the reasons we have indicated, one insists, eventually, on an elucidation of its constitutive elements. The danger then exists of giving the impression of a reduction of all religious life to this particular point and thus impoverishing it.

I. SOCIOLOGICAL DESCRIPTION OF RELIGIOUS LIFE

Let us begin our inquiry by taking an attentive and objective look at the concrete reality of religious life, just as it appears to any outsider. Religious life is not only an invisible mystery that can be perceived only by the eyes of faith; it is also a social reality sufficiently characterized so that one can describe it in its particulars. This social-empirical aspect does not by any means exhaust its reality, to be sure, but it does set us on a sure line of direction.

To attempt to describe religious life in this fashion is not easy — not so much because of its variety (most of its basic traits are the same everywhere) but because of its mobility and changeability. Many elements which served to define it yesterday, are today put into question and often abandoned.

Thus, religious dress which often set apart and designated a man or woman as a religious is in the process of disappearing completely for men, and more and more so for women. This results in the religious no longer being perceived as such individually but in reference to a community and style of life which he or she shares.

This style still appears greatly different from that of ordinary men and women. Religious often live in buildings built especially for them (rather spacious, compared to ordinary houses), and they lead a rather special life there. Similar in some respects to a boarding house or a hotel (relative isolation, impersonal atmosphere), these houses are nevertheless marked by a strict domestic order (a schedule, community exercises) in which prayer has an important place. What especially differentiates this life is that it is unisexual; we live in common exclusively with those of the same sex. The activity of the religious appears linked either to the house itself (menial labor) or institutions which it manages (teaching, health care, or social services), or the service of the Church (various ministries).

Such a life is structured by commitments (vows); the religious is perceived as someone who has publicly decided to lead this life in a permanent way and this decision confers upon him or her in the eyes of others a kind of setting apart. The most distinctive element of this setting apart is the fact of not being married, that is to say, celibacy vowed for religious motivations. Community of goods is another; as for poverty, one cannot say that it is usually perceived by others.

These are the aspects, in sketch form to be sure, under which religious life appears to the outside observer: men and women celibates living together in unisexual groupings, for religious motives, exercising activities usually at the service of the Church.

It is true, as we have indicated earlier, that this image is in the process of changing. The style of life as well as the work commitments are tending in another direction. What remains is the common life based on celibacy, and religious motivation expressed especially in prayer.

II. SPECIFIC NATURE OF RELIGIOUS LIFE IN THE MIDST OF CHRISTIAN LIFE

To be sure, the sociological approach has given us but a superficial view of the phenomena; above all, it has not answered the question of a specific nature.

Religious life, it goes without question, cannot be understood except within the framework of a Christian vocation. All that applies to the latter — the Gospel, its content of revelation and its radical demands, open-ended commitment in faith, constant questioning of oneself and of situations (*metanoia*) — obviously apply to it. Where, then, is the originality of religious life? What gives it its unique character; what makes it a vocation irreducible to another?

Various answers of unequal importance arise which can not even be classified as themes for discussion. For this reason we must systematize the diffuse views to serve our present needs, even at the risk of over-simplification.

1. Functional viewpoint.

According to this point of view, religious life has appeared in various moments of history in response to a specific need of the Church or the world which it tried to serve.[14] Thus, in the fourth century, monasticism sought to affirm without compromise a Christianity which was in danger of becoming too worldly; religious families appearing later sought to respond to various needs: evangelization, theological reflection, military aid, teaching, health care, etc. Since it was necessary to organize these movements for real efficiency, they were heavily structured (internal frameworks, commitment for life), and one adopted a type of life totally oriented to the realization of these undertakings. Celibacy, community of goods, and obedience, which are human as well as Christian possibilities, were assumed in this manner within the organization as means of attaining the objectives more easily. This was not accomplished without, to a certain extent, making these concepts absolute; moreover, the groups themselves, born for needs which were often temporary, sought to perpetuate themselves rather than disappear. Hence, the situation today of a multitude of disparate orders and congregations, all more or less identical, but seeking to affirm themselves in their diversity in order to provide for themselves a reason for existence.

From this perspective, the future of religious life appears linked with its pragmatic utility. Needs today are changing, but they certainly exist in sufficient number to stimulate commitments. The Third World and pioneer work in theological and social services are examples of the various areas in which Christians can render service. It is normal and often necessary that such objectives be proposed to the generosity of Christians. But is it necessary today that all these services be linked to celibacy, community of goods, and similar demands? Is not the service undertaken the essential matter, with all else having value in relation to it? This would result in a group with a structure firmly oriented toward the objective and the work to be done. Personal life would be left to the free decision of each.

As a possible proposal for the future, such a vision has nothing unacceptable in itself. After all, one can very well imagine men and women, married or single, committing themselves for a time or for life in a particular organization, as long as this affords them possibilities for self-realization and service. It is still true in our day that many needs have met no response, and that Christians will find underdeveloped fields ready for work everywhere.

But, aside from the fact that the idea of the apostolate or Church-directed service is, to say the least, strongly challenged (would Christians not be better placed in the service of so many already existing organizations?), a more basic objection is raised.

Granted that one need not reject such a conception in itself, neither does one have the right to reduce religious life to this end. Both history and reflection on the fact and the motives of commitment to the religious state are opposed to this.

Let us admit the existence of such "functional" religious groups, to begin with. There have been some in history; on the male side they were oriented towards efficient and regulated exercise ("canonical") of the sacerdotal ministry; on the feminine side, from the sixteenth century, they have taken on educational as well as charitable tasks.

Without saying that we have an exception here — in fact, most women's congregations of modern times are functional — one must nevertheless recognize that the most traditional (monastic) and most original forms of religious life, whether ancient or modern, do not fall into this category. One need only to read the rules of Pachomius, Basil, Augustine, Benedict, Francis of Assisi, Ignatius of Loyola, or Charles de Foucauld to become aware that these men sought above all to live a certain type of Christian life. They assign no functions to the brothers, no particular work in the Church or among men: they describe a life. The structures which one does find there, the Gospel demands — the three "counsels" usually occupy a rather modest place in relation to the whole, for example, in relation to the demands of prayer and mutual love — do not have the purpose of facilitating an activity; they are part of a certain style of life adopted gratuitously, for itself.

Moreover, one would have a hard time, studying history, saying to what concrete necessity of their times these groups responded; or, again, what activity was exclusive to them. It is true to say that they sought to renew Christian life, but if that is a function, it is valid for all Christians and always remains relevant.

We have already conceded that a number, sufficiently important perhaps, of communities come under the category said to be "functional." And it is possible that these communities will soon find themselves under the obligation of providing an answer to questions analagous to those raised previously. One thinks, for example, of the case of the Immaculate Heart Sisters of Los Angeles, typical in this respect;[15] a few congregations might be led to identical solutions. But it is foreseeable that even in these groups many religious will refuse reduction to simple functionalism. Certainly, reconciling gratuity — a life lived for itself — with a precise functional orientation will not be easy; perhaps it is even an impossible task. But the fact remains that some think they can live the two at the same time.

According to the functional viewpoint, the important thing is the task to be accomplished; the commitment rests on it. All else counts only in relationship to the task, and can be modified in consequence. However, in religious life as it has been lived to the present day, the opposite view has prevailed. The essential was always life lived in community, in celibacy, with the common sharing of goods and mutual submission; profession committed one to this life. To accept a functional orientation devalues the commitment and relativizes it. In fact, when the task no longer exists, the commitment loses its reason for existence. As far as celibacy, life in community, or the other demands are concerned, it is clear that they are not necessary to accomplish a specific task. Reduced to a functional character apart from itself, religious life is emptied of substance.

2. "Religious" viewpoint.

As the functional perspective gives to religious life a rather short-sighted utilitarian viewpoint in the "secular" line (it is a matter above all of accomplishing tasks of a social order), we are now concerned with a religious image.[16]

Religious life (speaking here mostly of monastic life, as we will see later) is characterized by certain values: retreat from the world, asceticism, and a cult of the interior life. It is, in the language used by Christians, the *fuga mundi*, penance, contemplation. Now these values are part of the religious dimension of man and are found, with more or less intensity, in every one of us. The great world religions have sought to promote them; in their midst, groups have existed, and continue to exist, whose purpose is to develop and organize this tendency, to make of it a "monastic" life. Such is the case for Hinduism, Buddhism and, in the West, Judaism (Qumran, the Essenes), and Christianity. To seek a place apart from the passing world, to tear oneself from men and their agitations, to live a chaste and frugal life (although, occasionally, one must recognize, asceticism lost its balance and expressed itself in ambiguous and spectacular ways), to devote oneself to meditation to which all else is subordinated — these are constant traits found in all these world religions. Heir to Judaism and influenced, perhaps, by oriental currents (a hypothesis which remains to be proven historically), Christianity offers an extremely favorable field for the blossoming and development of monasticism. Appearing first of all in its solitary and domestic form (the masculine and feminine *"parthenoi"* of the first three centuries), monasticism found its period of growth during the fourth century in cenobitic or eremitic colonies. Even if it was linked more to "religion" rather than "faith" under the form of Christian revelation, it had no trouble being accepted and ratified by the Church. Then, as a universal value, monasticism was adopted by the Church after being refashioned by the Gospel.

As mentioned previously, this schema is applicable in the first instance to the historical phenomenon of monasticism, granted that the latter wittingly defined itself by values such as retreat from the world, asceticism, and contemplation. But since all religious life finds its roots more or less in this primitive movement, it inserts itself willy-nilly in the same category. So much, then, for this thesis as it is proposed.

One can raise many serious objections to such a view of things which adduces mostly historical data. More than the functional view, this interpretation places the origin and the originality of this form of life outside of Christianity. Religious life would not be a Christian fact, but the assumption by the Church of a value existing elsewhere. Certainly, such an hypothesis has nothing unacceptable in itself; still, one would have to show this to be a reality supported by the facts. Now, nothing is less sure than the existence of Jewish monasticism; in any case, the Old Testament does not know it, and the Qumran community gives us data far too fragmentary for one to conclude that it had dependencies.

As for Buddhist monasticism, one must beware of identifying it too quickly with its Christian parallel because of certain resemblances. It is true that this phenomenon (likewise in Hinduism) has spiritual as well as numerical importance. But its history and concrete structure are little known to us; before making parallels showing resemblances and differences one would have to consult further studies which are lacking.[17] What is clear in any case is that the central project of monastic Buddhism is the fleeing and rejection of an illusory world with the purpose of attaining liberation of the self through illumination. One understands then how the abandonment of the world, liberating asceticism, and the search for interior life absolutely impose themselves; and this, in the name of a deep-seated dualism. If this is an accurate description of the heart of the Buddhist movement, one can speak only with difficulty of a relationship or affinities with Christian religious life unless one is willing to stop with superficial comparisons.

Moreover, one need only examine these values, even cursorily, to realize that, for as much as they do exist in Christianity, they have a far different meaning in the oriental traditions than one would like to attribute to them.

A certain capacity for retirement in relation to the world, a zone of solitude where one can enter into oneself and open oneself to mystery are human as well as Christian needs. Christ himself sojourned in the desert and slipped away to it in order to pray (Mk. 1, 35). But this is not rejection nor scorn of the world considered as essentially evil. The same is true for celibacy. The startling thing is that, as a religious *datum,* the latter flourishes almost exclusively in Christianity and Buddhism. But, aside from the fact that in the latter case it does not have the same modality, the meaning which one attaches to it is profoundly different. It rests, in fact, on the dualism of body/soul and on the notion that sexuality is a force, if not explicitly destructive, at least in the service of an illusory world.

As far as asceticism is concerned, it is a matter of mastery of self, interior as well as exterior, of victory over surrender and slavery to instincts; here again, a fundamental value, presupposed and demanded by Christianity. But in the oriental traditions, one finds an asceticism of more or less spectacular feats, or of performances of morbid self-destruction, having nothing to do with the Gospel, even if one does find a similar asceticism here and there also in Christian tradition. Finally, there is a distinction to be made between the search for the interior life and Christian prayer. Making oneself silent, opening oneself to the mystery of life, touching the depths of one's life — these are part of a fundamentally human dimension and can obviously contribute to prayer. But the latter is something else: presence — or at least desire for presence — to the absolute mystery which is a personal God who calls men by his historical revelation in Christ. It is not the search for oneself, but an opening of oneself to the other. Thus, these elements which one might claim derive from elsewhere and which one would want to make proper to religious life, are either absent from this life (at least in the form found in non-Christian monasticism), or lived according to a different signification; but they are part of the Gospel and then of all Christian existence. To reduce monasticism (and with it all forms of Christian life) to natural religious values appears to us as a possibly interesting hypothesis (it supplies, in effect, a certain clarification), but one without much foundation.

3. Christian perspectives.

The viewpoints discussed until now, which see in religious life a functional response to certain needs of the Church and, above all, society, or which look upon it as an expression of a religious attitude of man, have nothing specifically Christian about them. Indeed, if one pursues their logic to the end one would have to conclude, either that religious life is an adventitious phenomenon, circumstantial and without gospel roots, or that it is a general human value which Christianity adopted, certainly, but which it did not originate.

Now, right or wrong, through a long history the Christian conscience has seen, to the contrary, a distinctive gospel manifestation in religious life. On this point, the testimony of "rules" — texts expressing form of a way of life — is explicit and unanimous. Since the texts of Pachomius, all the rules — those of Basil, Benedict, Francis, Charles de Foucauld, Taizé — intend themselves to be rooted in the gospel and propose nothing but a radical fidelity to the call addressed by Christ to all believers. The men and women who, in the course of centuries, have committed themselves to religious life believed that they were doing so in the name of the demands of Christian life, starting from those demands and not from some outside influence or pragmatic need. Certainly, even in this case, a critical view can legitimately analyze the presuppositions and unconscious choices, but it is forced to take into account the clearly affirmed gospel project.

All the more so since reflection on the state of life in the Church, from the beginning to our day, has always maintained the link between the phenomenon of religious life and its gospel origins. Thus, the awareness this life has of itself, along with the vision theology maintains, point to the Christian originality of the phenomenon of religious life.

Without attempting to settle immediately the question of depth — the pages which follow will bring, we hope, some answer — let us analyze the various theological approaches to religious life. How is this life situated within the general Christian vocation of which it is considered an integral part? Such a question deserves, first of all, an historical study; in fact, the understanding we have of religious life, the explanation given to it, varies with the centuries. But a work which would provide such a study of the history of religious life remains to be undertaken, and it reaches beyond the possibilities of this modest reflection.

More simply, one can expose and discuss a few concepts which are current today. This is a matter of theological views and synthesis, not the analysis of rules; the latter, without doubt, would yield a far richer image, but would be less formulated into subjects for discussion.

(a) *Perfectionist concepts.*

We face a question here of a perspective clearly in decline, one which is less and less proposed or defended explicitly. Nevertheless, since it was dominant not so long ago, it continues to impregnate many studies of religious life. One need only subject certain expressions to some scrutiny to see traces appear of the old concept of religious life as the perfection of Christian life.

This concept finds expression in many ways. It presupposes as a point of departure the distinction between precepts and counsels in the teachings of Jesus. The former are imposed on all Christians and assure them of salvation; the latter are invitation, callings introducing one to the way of perfection. The three counsels of poverty, chastity, and obedience are the essential means to this perfection.

In a more disinterested and less impersonal fashion the same idea appears in the theme of closer imitation of Christ, in the act of being his "disciple," in the stricter sense of that word. Those who renounce their goods, committing themselves to celibacy and obedience, follow Christ more closely, as did the first disciples. They therefore compose a particular category, analogous to the restricted group which surrounded Jesus during his historical existence.

The idea, more recently advanced, of a special consecration to God — something not strictly of Scriptural origin — seems to fall in the same category. Taken in an objective sense — a consecrated man or woman is given to God and his service — consecration confers on the Christian making this religious commitment a special setting apart for God. He or she appears in relation to other Christians as a sacred being belonging more strictly to God.

The perfectionist concept traced here in its essentials has been criticized and refuted time and time again. It is therefore unnecessary to dwell at length on it. One need only point out that the teaching of the New Testament does not recognize two categories of Christians, some called to the common way, others to perfection. The distinction between precepts and counsels, at least in the sense that some are obligatory and others optional and addressed only to a few, has long ago been denounced as without foundation. If it is true, as we will see throughout this study, that religious life does not hold up without a continued effort of fidelity to the gospel, without the desire to go all the way with its demands, then, certainly, this effort is equally valid for all authentic Christian life.

As a state of life, religious life has this demand inscribed in its very heart. But does it differ in this from the aim of Christian life itself?

(b) Gospel radicalism.

Rejecting the idea of finding particular texts in the New Testament which justify the existence of religious life and explain its meaning, this approach attributes the originality of this life to the radicalism with which the Christian life is lived.[18] It is an absolute and categorical way of living a common vocation of following Christ, a desire to accept the gospel calling in an energetic and clear-cut fashion.

It is true that evangelical perfection is proposed without distinction to all believers; therefore, all must take the necessary means, even radical and absolute, each time the situation requires. This is the sense in which one must understand the invitation to take up one's cross every day (Lk. 9, 23), to renounce oneself (Mt. 16, 24), to hate one's father and mother (Lk. 14, 24), to sell all that one has (Lk. 14, 33), to cut off one's hand or pluck out the eye which is a source of scandal (Mt. 5, 29-30), to live as a eunuch (Mt. 19, 12).

But in imitating the life led by the group who followed Jesus, the religious commits himself or herself to a state where the radical attitude becomes the norm, the internal law that is institutionalized. Thus the originality of the religious life does not rest on the fact that it would manifest a partial aspect of the Christian vocation (such as its eschatological character, or a different type of insertion in the world), but in the fact that it takes seriously, absolutely, and unconditionally the demands of Christ, not only in boundary situations (where they are imposed on all believers), but as a habitual state. By this it reveals what is central in Christianity: the receptiveness of faith, the radical availability to the Word pronounced in Christ.

This view commands very solid arguments, exegetical and historical, as a basis.

In fact, it is generally admitted that no Scriptural texts exist which could establish a certain type of Christian life (with the exception, however, of celibacy, to which we will return). The religious life refers, then, to the totality of the gospel demands, as does all of Christian life. As a matter of fact, an analysis of the different rules shows that this has been so historically.[19] It is not one or the other practical aspect which is given a privileged status in them, but the entire gospel proposed in explicit terms. Thus, the rules of Basil and Augustine set as a point of departure the double commandment of love, and the Benedictine Rule invites the monk to enter upon a road that has the gospel for its guide. Francis of Assisi affirms that the life and rule of the friars consist in observing the holy gospel of Christ, and he cites the strength of its radical demands: sell all that you have and give it to the poor (Mt. 19, 21); prefer Christ to those near to you, even over your own life (Lk. 14, 26).

Historical evidence shows that all great religious families are born in a climate of gospel radicalism. The men and women at the origin of these movements desired one thing only for themselves and their companions: to live the adventure of their faith in Jesus Christ with all its consequences. This was the heart of their religious project, nothing else. They had no functional or religious purpose, proposed no theoretical vision, spoke very little of celibacy; their purpose was to live in a bold and clear-cut way their Christian vocation.

One can but state one's agreement with this presentation which shows, from the gospel and from history, the focal point of religious life.

Yet questions remain, the first being of the historical order: Can one seriously affirm that gospel radicalism, in the sense described above, actually identifies itself *concretely* with the concrete phenomenon of religious life? Is it not more extensive? In other words, has this radicalism been lived exclusively within this sociological group called religious life? One can certainly refuse to identify religious life with the forms which history and the law have delineated, but then one becomes involved in a very vaguely defined zone, where it is difficult to get hold of anything. If all the Christians who live this radical way of life are religious, how is it possible to distinguish those for whom this name has been reserved in the course of history? Moreover, sad to say, one is aware that this radicalism has been realized, even in the midst of religious life, by only a small number. Would the mark of a religious be only the resolution, the "state," in which one commits oneself to radicalism? But how would the condition of the ordinary Christian be different? Does not every believer who takes his faith seriously also commit himself to a total response to his calling?

Another objection presents itself: Such a viewpoint seems to introduce, in a divisive way, the notion of two categories or classes of Christians. Certainly, among believers there are those who try to live fully their new situation in the face of their weakness, and there are others — perhaps the greater number — who live in inattention and mediocrity. But where does the demarcation line cut across? Can one say that religious life (whatever the sociological extension one wishes to give such a term) constitutes the real division? Who would dare affirm it? Does not such an affirmation return to the doctrine of religious life as a state of perfection?

Another difficulty remains, that of the very notion of radicalism and its possible form as an institution. What is "gospel radicalism"? Is it simply a matter of a certain number of Jesus' words, reported primarily by the Synoptics (such as the admonitions to sell everything, leave those near to us, behave as eunuchs, allow oneself to be stripped, renounce oneself, carry one's cross, etc.), a few of which can be observed to the letter? Would not the depth of this sort of radicalism be, rather, the demand to prefer faith in Jesus Christ and the love of men and women to oneself, to others, to the entire world? Do not both John and Paul, who do not report the words quoted previously, say the same thing when they speak to us of the necessity of coming to Christ, of believing in him without reference to oneself, of sharing in faith in his life and resurrection? Briefly, is it not faith itself that has a certain coefficient of radicalism? Does not the person who begins to say yes to the Word of Christ necessarily commit himself or herself to a process of total self-transcendence, of a coming-out of self, of a death which opens up on a new birth? The words which the Synoptics report, while often paradoxical, are they not, rather than a literal exigency, the terse remembrance of a commitment in faith to the Lord's death and resurrection, a constant break from and refusal of a settled situation?

Is it not a certain exaggeration to speak of radicalism as becoming a norm and institution? Certainly, the spiritual texts which established the various forms of religious life recall with emphasis the *logia* of the Lord, considering them to express this radicalism. The texts suggest them as stimulants and as ideals. Can one at the same time say that these words are proposed as concrete norms, juridically formulated? It is so for celibacy and for a certain number of words related to the community of goods; for example, the selling and distribution of goods (Mk. 10, 20) and the literal acceptance of the missionary discourse (Mt. 9-10: take no money, no sandals, only one tunic). Only Francis of

Assisi proposed these demands as concrete gestures. We see the difficulty, then, of proposing the totality of "radical" texts — excepting those mentioned above — as constituting norms or laws for religious, over and above all other Christians. In other words, are Christians who do not fit into the category of "religious" any less linked to this gospel radicalism?

Schematizing briefly, one could say that religious life degenerates and becomes a dead institution when it is no longer animated by the will to follow the gospel all the way; or, if you wish, to follow gospel radicalism. In this sense, radicalism is at the very heart of this life as a basic basis that is taken for granted. But one must beware of monopolizing this radicalism at the expense of what is the sociological institution of religious life, for it belongs to the Christian faith itself, and then to all Christians who adhere to Jesus Christ.

While admitting the extreme importance — even more, the central place — of this theme, I don't think it alone is sufficient to express the specific nature of the religious vocation. For, this vocation cannot have as its basis any common demand of the Christian faith as such, which would be valid, consequently, for every man and woman taking this faith seriously.

(c) *An aspect of the Christian vocation.*

Refusing to situate the originality of religious life in its pursuit of individual perfection or to consider it the exclusive repository of gospel radicalism (even though it could not exist otherwise), we can more accurately describe it as a partial and secondary aspect of the Christian life. It is more important to be Christian; to be religious is only a possibility for living the Christian vocation. The "Christian" type is everything; the "specific difference," minimal of itself, is important when making distinctions.

But where does the difference lie? Not in points and demands addressed to all Christians, which each believer must try to introduce into his or her life as well as possible. The religious life is the place where free possibilities are presented; not the counsels of perfection, but meaningful choices for a certain type of existence quite apart from the viewpoint of perfection and salvation.

What differentiates religious life from the life of the lay Christian is celibacy, chosen for Christ and before the whole Church, as a definitive and public state of life. From that point, due to its positive dynamism which is creative of universal relationships and a source of community, celibacy introduces a new type of existence into the Church and the world, a complementary pole to lay life.

Since this subject has already been more amply examined in a previous study, and in the following chapters we will discuss its Scriptural foundations and meaning, I present here only a synthetic general view. The pole in question here is not a particular reference to God, Jesus Christ, or his gospel. This reference is identical for all Christians, who must all live radically, albeit in different ways. The reality distinguishing religious from non-religious life is not of a vertical (man to God in Christ) but horizontal (man to other men and women) order.[20] Celibacy, chosen in faith ("for the Lord," "for the kingdom," and hence on the "vertical" dimension, if one wishes) nevertheless possesses a deeply human meaning. It does not change the person's relationship to God, but that of the man or woman to others, particularly to one of the opposite sex as an eventual partner, to whom one in principle refuses oneself. For the man or woman committed to it, it creates a new situation, another type and possible network of human relations. It allows — one almost says, requires — an original community, different from the familial or any other type of community.

Now the relational level, where one situates both marriage and celibacy, is an absolutely fundamental phase of human existence. If marriage is the prevailing fact, almost the norm, the reality of a successful celibacy is at once an affirmation of freedom and the sign of a possible future for men and women. Linked to faith, since it leans on a possibility and a promise affirmed by the Word of God, celibacy introduces on the "horizontal" level of existence a newness which reflects on all dimensions of human life. Normally, adult individuals are inserted in social, economic, and political structures as couples. The existence of men and women living in society without being part of its fundamental structure — i.e., the couple — is first of all an original sociological fact, especially if accompanied, as it usually is, by the existence of a strongly structured community.

This original human reality then possesses an intramundane relational significance at the same level as the other phase of life, even while initially appearing to deny it. But, because at the beginning it rests on a decision of faith to which it must constantly refer to endure — contrary to marriage, which is a phase of nature — it carries a second, distinctly Christian meaning.

Therefore, religious life, like lay life, is situated on the level of relationship to others; but it affirms the universality of this relation by going beyond the exclusive sexual link.

Otherwise, it is not fundamentally different, neither on the level of human life nor Christian vocation. Certainly, proceeding from the fundamental rupture constituting celibacy and the extension of relationships which it allows, concrete life can take on original aspects. Domestic life, professional activity, and religious acts are marked by particular traits; a different polarity, a different complementary and reciprocal state exist. But the fact remains the same.

The schematic view proposed here (to be developed in the following pages) will appear to be a reduction. Is religious life simply a more or less profane celibacy tied to a functional community? This understanding of celibacy would be contrary to all this study wishes to clarify. Like Christian existence, religious life is submitted to the demands of the gospel, and these, as we shall see, impose themselves with a special urgency. But its special image, its uniqueness, consists in one, important but secondary element. To seek a definition of religious life by reserving to it exclusively something which lies at the heart of the gospel would, with one blow, reduce the level of the Christian vocation in general.

Chapter III

RELIGIOUS LIFE AND CHRISTIAN RESPONSIBILITY

In the eyes of Christians, and, often, in the eyes of religious themselves, religious life has appeared, and still appears, as a sort of "super-Christian" life. Most of its constitutive elements — prayer, asceticism, poverty, obedience, community, not to mention celibacy — are considered the exclusive reserve of this life. The religious who are faithful to these demands is considered a man or woman of God, a consecrated one, a "specialist" in Christian life. He or she does better, and more, than others; his or her life is organized completely around the Gospel. From these images comes the idea that here is a vocation altogether "special": proper to some and of no concern to others. It is only a short step to this conclusion, and this step is quickly taken.

Even today, when the idea of a general calling spoken to the whole body of the faithful is readily admitted, some continue to think that the practice of frequent prayer or the common sharing of goods are demands proper only to religious life. The consequence is that non-religious Christians, believing themselves unaffected by these demands, feel dispensed from their practice.

As far as the religious is concerned, he often has no objection to being regarded as a specialist in prayer and poverty. There is, thus, on the one hand a monopoly or annexation ("this is *our* vocation"), and on the other, an acceptance of the exigencies of ordinary Christian life, with its consequent impoverishment ("this does not concern us").

It is an undeniable historical fact that religious life — in law and in fact — is a Christian life having a certain intensity. But, granting this, does it mean that they live an ideal inaccessible to others, a sort of luxury? Or do they practice what is required of everyone? In other words, by reserving, in theory and in practice, the radicalism of the gospel (such as it is expressed in prayer, asceticism, the common life, etc.) to religious alone, is not the lay Christian life reduced to a sort of mediocrity, or, to say the least, to an "honest" middle way?

Our task is not to reduce the demands of religious life, bringing them down to the smallest common denominator, but, rather, to affirm anew that gospel radicalism addresses itself to all, and that the values professed and lived by religious, for better or worse, are values which must be held in all Christian living.

Examining a certain number of points, we will try to demonstrate the identity of these two vocations. Certain values are effectively lived by all Christians desiring to go the limit with their faith. Such is the case for asceticism, obedience, chastity, etc.; others appear proper only to religious: frequent prayer, poverty, and community. The point is, is this normal, is it not a false orientation for Christianity? The responsibility for this state of affairs falls not only on religious — happy as they are to be placed on a pedestal — but on lay people as well — happy as they may be in shirking the demands common to all.

We will form our answer, first of all, by analyzing not the theoretical viewpoints, but the reality such as it is lived. This will permit us to demythologize certain excessively facile declarations, and to point out the true demands.

I. PRIMACY OF THE GOSPEL

We say, and often write, that one of the characteristics of the religious life is the subordination and total orientation of structure to the gospel and its demands. It is a human life, certainly, with various functions — eating, drinking, working, resting, relating, etc. — but all of this is subordinate to its central aim: to live the faith in God and in Jesus Christ, to love and to serve men and women. Its very principle of organization, encompassing the whole of life and holding first priority, is this design of faith. It would not be so for the lay person; in this lies the difference.

At the level of first impressions, these things correspond well to reality. The rules of religious orders are polarized, in effect, by the design of placing faith and love at the center of religious existence: "to desire nothing but the Spirit of the Lord and his holy operation" (Francis). Effectively, as soon as religious life achieves a certain authenticity the desire to live these values is re-grasped and reaffirmed unceasingly. One seeks, by solitude, prayer, and structured service of one's neighbor, to create a favorable setting for this spiritual desire.

But what of the Christian life outside the structures of religious life? The impression is received that the life of the community, as such, is reduced to a very few things: the weekly Eucharistic assembly and the invitation to join its fellowship; the remainder is left to the good will and the capabilities of each. The Christian life of the individual, lived most often in the traditional family structure, carries almost no exterior demand, except perhaps family prayer, which is very rare.

In speaking thus, we may appear to suppose that any structuring of life based on the gospel is principally expressed by cultural acts. One could object by saying that it is precisely lay life which expresses this structuring in another way, by intending to orient everything towards God; or, in more secularized language, by adopting these tasks purely for their own value. But even in proposing such an interpretation, we presuppose as something taken for granted that the whole life of the believer must be organized in one way or another around this center of unity which is faith in Jesus Christ.

Whatever the case — whether absolute subordination to the gospel must be expressed by particular acts, or by an intention attendant to all action, or even by both at once — it appears evident that all Christian life worthy of the name will always place its reference to the gospel at its heart. On this point, we cannot speak of different vocations. One can only respond, more or less well, to this unique calling.

If it is true that the religious community organizes all the elements of its life in a visible way around the gospel, and that lay Christians seem to live an existence less polarized by the faith, we should realize that this is due to many factors.

First of all, there is a lack, perhaps, of clearsightedness in such a view of things. One forgets that the primacy of the gospel consists, in the first place, in a constantly-renewed faith which remains at the base of one's existence. Even if this is not visibly expressed — so the question continually arises: how should this subordination be expressed? — it is still, perhaps, a life totally based on faith. It still remains, however, that faith is not a purely interior option, without any real impact on all the depths of concrete life. If one organizes everything around this fundamental axis, this must be realized. And if such apparently is not the case with lay life, there are many reasons accounting for it. In a society which is pluralistic from the viewpoint of faith — and this begins to be more and more true for family society as well — it is difficult, if not impossible, to impose values or to organize life around criteria which are not shared by all. This is certainly one real disadvantage for lay life in its natural structures (domestic, professional, social) as opposed to religious life.

But the true Christian community is not necessarily, nor always, the milieu of family, professional, social, or political life. Faith — while respecting these realities — often shatters such frames of reference: "who are my brothers, my sisters, my mother, but those who do the will of the Father?" (Mk. 3, 35). So this question is posed to the Christian community — the Church — at the heart of which the Christian lives his faith. Does this community create a milieu of life and faith where in fact all is subordinate to the gospel? And the question extends beyond the individual Christian to the ecclesial community. Can this, perhaps, be less structured around the gospel than, in theory and —

thank God — often in practice, the religious life? If this often happens, is it not through dullness and dislocation?

This reflection, rather general in character, receives a greater clarification if we analyze a certain number of elements one usually considers expressive of life according to the gospel.

II. PRAYER

Christian prayer — whether private or communal — is the privileged manifestation of faith. Through it, faith is confessed and celebrated; it is the most important, perhaps the only, place where the specific nature of the Christian reality is expressed. There has not been and there will never be a Christianity without worship which is prayer.

In religious life, prayer in both its forms occupies a choice place, as a project and as a reality. While prayer "seven times a day" (as was the practice from the fourth and fifth centuries until recently) is no longer common, two or three moments of common prayer each day and periods of solitary prayer still remain in current practice. This is, at any rate, what seems to differentiate religious from lay Christians.

The latter, for the most part, are content with the Sunday Eucharist; private prayer in the morning and evening seems to be on the way out, not to mention family prayer, which has always been fairly rare. It is therefore all the more surprising to note a certain renewal of common prayer (in small, spontaneous groups), either regular or sporadic, as well as the abundance of Christians in places where a living and joyous prayer is celebrated. And this, at the very time when religious, reacting against a structure of prayer which was too heavy or through a desire to be like other Christians, question the importance of regular and frequent prayer.

One should carefully question whether daily prayer is proper to religious life exclusively, or if it should not be a fundamental requirement of the whole Christian community. Should not that which religious life has preserved, in spite of its incrustations and deformities, be the common vocation of everyone? In reserving prayer to religious and, later, to priests, in establishing them as "official delegates" or surrogates, have we not done a grave disservice to the entire Christian community, by allowing them to consider themselves dispensed from this effort?

In fact, from the testimony of the first centuries (Tertullian, Hippolytus),[21] we see that it is the whole Christian community (at least in principle) which takes part in the celebration of prayer, once or twice a day; not to speak of the times advised for private or household prayer. The monks of the fourth century did not pretend to do more or better than the others. At the moment when a massive and superficial Christianization was lowering the general level of Christian life, they saw themselves pursuing what had always been the practice of the community. Rather than a wish to do more or to set aside a privileged aspect of the Christian life, it was a reaction based on faith and fervor against a slackening of this life. Through the course of centuries and until our day, this fidelity has been maintained, and through this, above all, religious life manifests its eschatological character: the subordination of everything to that which is uniquely essential; but one sees in it much more a special vocation than the maintenance of a common requirement.

Today it is necessary to see the terms of the question clearly, and to weigh the consequences which follow from different responses. If frequent prayer is exclusive to religious life, are we not establishing a monopoly at the expense of the lay Christian — a monopoly on what the gospel says of prayer and is addressed to everyone? But if religious have preserved a practice which should never have ceased being a part of the life of the whole Christian community, then we face the need for a revision. Not, certainly, the need to fix new juridical obligations or to imagine that all Christians should come together for prayer twice a day. But one would at least need to affirm that this is a possible ideal, a normal thing, and at the same time to create concrete possibilities for common prayer wherever Christian communities exist or are beginning to grow. Is this an impossible dream?

While it remains true that religious life, due to its freedom in regard to certain structures, is able to carry out its responsibility for prayer more easily and, therefore, with greater faithfulness, in doing so it can make no claim to a special vocation or mission; it can only serve to remind all Christians of that to which all are invited.

III. ASCETICISM

The concept of "asceticism" is not of Christian but of Stoic origin. It refers to the detachment, the renunciation which one must impose on oneself to become free and master of oneself. Christianity has nevertheless quickly adopted both the word and the content, transforming it in the process. In fact, without mentioning the radical demands of Jesus on his disciples, demands requiring the abandonment and death of oneself to be totally open to the gospel, the question of the training a believer undertakes to remain faithful to his or her vocation already arises in the Pauline letters (1 Cor. 9, 24-27).

In Christian asceticism, as long as it remained authentic, there was always this element proper to it, namely, the link between, on the one hand, renunciation and the entry of men and women into the mystery of the death and resurrection of Christ, and on the other hand, practices and tendencies flowing from a concept of the human which did not always exclude a certain dualism.

From the beginning, monastic environments were marked by an austerity of life, even though the rules, in general, do not underline this as a central point of value. This situation has continued to exist practically until our day. Yet one must clarify what is at question here. There are, in fact, two meanings of the word asceticism.

The first, most general and fundamental, is that of mastery of self, of control, of training, which a person practices to become truly human, and, if Christian, to be more truly available to the call of the Gospel. This means dominating natural tendencies;

thus, mastery of self in eating and drinking, control of sexuality, moderation in rest and diversions. One must avoid dissipation, thoughtlessness, superficiality: hence the necessity of solitude, marking a certain distance from events, and of reflection favorable to depth and interior life. All efforts undertaken to live in this way, techniques for its eventual awakening and sustenance, are part of asceticism understood in this first sense.

The second sense is more specialized. It is a matter of ascetic or penitential practices, such as religious life has known for a long time and still knows even today in certain places. These customs include: cloister (separation from others, restriction and control of mobility, visits, and mail, material isolation of houses), silence, fasting, vigils (nocturnal common prayer), and other practices like sleeping on hard surfaces, wearing of rough garments, discipline, etc. If, to say the least, these practices were widespread in most religious families, one must realize that they have become a point of crisis today.

Except for monastic women (not absolutely in their case, either) and certain male communities, cloister is mostly a legal term rather than a felt reality. Fasting — something practiced by all Christians, and even more frequently by the monks — has become only a memory, even among most of the religious themselves. The penitential practices mentioned above have almost completely disappeared. One can deplore this, but one must recognize the fact.

To speak today of asceticism as a characteristic note, or even the proper vocation, of religious life would be an exaggeration if not a mystification, to say the least. It is evident that without asceticism taken in the first sense above, there can be no authentic human or Christian living. To take one's life in one's hands, to live deeply, to sustain silence and peace in oneself is as indispensable for a religious as any Christian, even for any human worthy of the name. More fundamentally, anyone who wishes to speak of the necessity of dying to oneself each day, as Christ did, in order to rise again with him, will entertain no doubt that we are confronted here with a fundamental Christian demand valid for everyone.

Speaking of asceticism in its second sense, we have just seen that this concept and its practice are in the process of undergoing a change which, at the moment, can be seen mostly from its negative side. The values which it carried — silence, nocturnal prayer, and even fasting — will, we hope, rediscover a renewed relevance, once they have been freed from legal formalism and rendered more spontaneous. One point above all appears most important to us: that of separation. Practically, this is a question of rediscovering a certain distance in relation to the rush and artificial character of urban life. To live in the country — not for good, but from time to time — is after all the dream of today's man or woman. While this dream is often colored by escapism — leaving the city, one discovers that one carries it within oneself — there is a tendency which marks a real evolution. What is valid in this dream is the concept of creating a lifestyle for men and women that is less inhuman, more simple, more free, and ultimately more conducive to interior life.

But all these values are human values which must be freed and made available to everyone, even if the religious life may have been more faithful to them than most Christians or other people.

IV. POVERTY

The practice of poverty figures among the three elements (counsels and vows) which are said to be distinctive of religious life. In fact, this is true historically, although one must make certain distinctions. While the community of goods appears in the Acts of the Apostles as a mark of the Church in Jerusalem (Acts 4, 37), it is not a question of poverty. Likewise for the rules of Basil, Augustine, and Benedict. In them mention is made of holding goods in common, even though, admittedly, this includes a modest and frugal life. Insistence on poverty (the word and the mystique) is found, on the contrary, in the rules of Francis of Assisi, where the demands of divesting oneself are radically affirmed: to sell one's goods and distribute the proceeds to the poor, to follow the letter of Matthew's gospel concerning clothing (10, 9 ff.), to refuse to handle money. Since the Middle Ages, the vocabulary and mystique of poverty have always had their place in the rules and constitutions ("to love poverty as a mother" are words from the *Constitutions of the Company of Jesus*).

It is a fact, then, that the different religious movements have always sought to hold everything in common and to live modestly, and certain currents — especially Franciscan — even went further on the road of radicalism. Each time, it was a matter of fidelity to the gospel and of reaction, conscious or not, to the wealth and established order of the Christian community. This was surely the case of monasticism in the fourth century, which wished to revive the ideal of the community at Jerusalem that was being neglected in the aftermath of the recognition of the Church by the Empire, when the Church had begun to profit materially from this alliance. Again with the evangelism of the twelfth and thirteenth centuries it was a reaction against the temporal power of the Church and the mounting affluence of Christians in general.

But what is the situation of poverty in religious life today? The fact that it is being talked about so much indicates that everything is not going so well. Religious (except for recent groups like the family of Charles de Foucauld) have a rather bad conscience on this point; in fact, they are reproached for having, in most cases, more-than-sufficient means (buildings, real estate, endowments, etc.). Certainly, all of this is at the service of the community and the Church, and individual lives are often very modest. But the appearances are not of "poverty"; the most one could say, in their defense, is that they are ordinary. Above all, while there is a community of goods internally, sharing with others outside is rare in practice.

Briefly, demythologizing the image of religious poverty and looking at the situation objectively, it must be admitted that without being a financial power, religious communities and religious today are not poor in the sociological sense of the world. They practice a community of goods which is an undeniably important fact. They usually live modestly, are content with a modest use of things, hold a certain freedom *vis-á-vis* economic and financial structures, and are not engaged in the pursuit of social status. It is not very convincing to call this poverty. But on the other hand, moderation, community of goods and a certain freedom are indeed values which deserve to be put into greater clarity.

Outside religious life the theme of poverty is not unknown either. It is true that, in general, poverty is not presented as a fundamental Christian demand. When this is done, it is given a spiritual interpretation: one must be poor in spirit, i.e., interiorly. It is noteworthy, however, that poverty is the order of the day in current renewal. Christians are generally very demanding of the Church, which they accuse of being rich and of holding sides with the powerful. They do not believe very much in the poverty of religious, either. At the same time it is true that few among them feel personally concerned with the gospel calling. We ask for a Church of the poor, without realizing that this is not possible without the commitment of all who constitute the Church to this way. However, there are exceptions; there are Christians who seek to discern the meaning of gospel poverty and to put it into practice. This shows that poverty too is not simply the monopoly of religious, but is proposed to all believers.

Such is surely, in fact, the meaning of the gospel call to poverty. It is, certainly, a demand which is above all interior: recognizing one's insufficiency and dependence before God, relying on him from whom everything comes, not the least of which is one's own being; becoming attentive and open to the free movement of God, who gives himself; keeping oneself in joyous thanksgiving for all that is given. But poverty necessarily expresses itself on the sociological plane. It is, then, a refusal to put one's heart and preoccupations into a search for riches or wealth; to have, rather, a certain mistrust of everything which alienates one from the other, and to have a desire to share which is concrete.

Transposed into contemporary situations and articulated in today's language, poverty is first of all sharing or the community of goods. Holding whatever one has in common, creating equality among individuals, social classes, nations (the problems of the Third World), this is the principle necessity. The Christian's vocation to poverty today means to be shocked by injustice, inequality, individual and collective egotism which thinks of nothing but itself, to fight socially and politically in order to reverse the *status quo*, accepting the price which must be paid, and to realize in the Christian community something of this broad vision.

It is also opposition to the situation created by the more economically advanced societies today. The Christian professing poverty according to the gospel refuses to enter the vicious circle of production and consumption without critique or resistance. He or she seeks a simple, unpretentious life, rejects an accumulating abundance which creates artificial needs, and is content with things which are honest, useful, and few in number. Often, at the call of the Spirit, such a Christian will manifest his or her freedom from oppressive structures by a prophetic gesture or action.

Should this be considered utopian? Is it not, on the contrary, a demand which is inscribed at the heart of the gospel? In neglecting to proclaim it as such to all, in reserving it as a special vocation of a restricted group, do we not risk proclaiming an insipid gospel? If the Church had always announced the gospel in these terms, presenting it as the ideal of all Christians, would not the face of the world be different today? Here again, religious life has practiced and conserved an aspect of the common Christian vocation. Today it is important that the same calling be perceived and put into practice by all believers.

V. OBEDIENCE

Would it not then be in obedience that one finds the particular character of religious life? A reading of the rules shows us, in fact, that the exercise of obedience occupies an important place in the common life. It is true that its concept and practice have known a long and complex evolution.

We begin to see an evolution already in the first well-documented cenobitic experience, that of Pacomius.[22] With Basil, who speaks of obedience at length, it is a matter in the first place of the fundamental obedience of the Christian: obey the gospel as Christ obeyed the Father — until death. Each Christian brother living in a community is a mediator of this obedience each time he causes the other to hear a demand of the Word. The one who is in charge of the community naturally finds his place within this image; all the more so, since, following the image of the body, there is a diversity of charisms in the body which is the community, and everything must go on in order and with good measure. The responsible one is a brother; he is the eye of the community, and he remains submissive to the control of his brothers. No particular name is given to him.[23]

In Augustine, obedience is more strongly tied to a central authority: he who holds authority is called father, and one must honor him. The Benedictine rule presents a very precise image of the abbot as vested with Christ's authority; it describes at length the qualities which must be his, as well as the manner of obedience of the brothers; it also speaks, however, of the mutual obedience of all. As for the text of Basil: the image of authority is more strong, more situated at the summit; the texts cited in speaking of it (Mt. 11, 29; Lk. 22, 27; I Th. 4, 7; Jn. 13, 34 and 15, 13) which are in reference to the humble service of fraternal love, are no longer used.

They are used, however, by Francis of Assisi. One feels in him a reaction — evangelical — against a certain concept of authority. The brothers will have neither father nor prior, they will all be "lesser brothers." The brother charged with the service of all will be called servant, and he must constantly be on his guard against all temptations to power and domination. Though everyone must obey him in what is not contrary to the rule or conscience, he is subject to their control. All must manifest a mutual obedience of love towards one another.

The concept of Ignatius of Loyola, often presented as militaristic, centralist, and absolutist, is more full of nuances than generally realized. The fact remains that it has shaped the concept of authority in most groups, old or new, according to the sixteenth century model. This concept, which has not always kept the Ignatian equilibrium, sees the superior as the principle if not unique mediator of the will of God in the life of each one. The orders and wishes of the superior, if not contrary to the objective conscience of the subject, must be received and carried out as manifestations of the divine will.

Through this evolution it appears, on the one hand, that there was a strengthening of authority as experience progressed; on the other, at least with Francis, a gospel criticism of authority as it was currently exercised. It is obvious that concepts of authority are modeled on contemporary sociological forms, whether one likes it or not: the abbot of the Benedictine rule has something of the role of the *paterfamilias* of Roman Christianity. The religious superior of the seventeenth or eighteenth century resembles a more or less absolute monarch. On this point, one would help to sift out the evangelical values from their sociological conditioning.

All the more so today, since the practice and theological justification for obedience are questioned in what is occasionally a radical way. There is discussion of the evangelical bases of religious obedience; in fact, they cannot be found exegetically. Contemporary society, of which religious are a part, contests any authority acting in isolation, without participation and without democratic discussion — authority which holds any rank other than that of servant. While granting the ideal of order and interdependence, and, consequently, of a service of unity or even decision for a group, the idea of submitting oneself gratuitously to another is repugnant. Whether it is a question of obedience to the gospel and its demands, of interdependence, or of coordination and order, does not this hold for all Christians, and even for all men and women?

It is from this point of view that it is good to examine the question raised at the beginning of this chapter on obedience: that is to say, whether religious live a reality different from other Christians in this regard.

When it is a matter of hearing the word of God which comes from Jesus Christ through the testimony of the Apostles and the life of the Church, one must obey the example of Christ, even if this means facing death itself. Here is a fundamental necessity: obedience and belief are two different words expressing the same reality. Understood in the concrete life of each believer, such obedience encompasses his or her particular vocation as a man or woman and as a Christian. Here again, although the field of application will be more flexible and more relative, the same necessity holds sway.

If one wishes to speak of inter-human relationships and obedience — although the word love would be more *apropos* here — this can only be expressed as the duty of each one to listen to the other, to accept him or her, be sensitive to the other's important requests, and to allow the other a certain space where he or she can live and affirm his or her own way. This is a central datum of human relations, which is called mutual love in the gospels and in early letters of the Church. Without it, neither true rapport nor the communal dimension can exist. Such a demand is valid for every person, for their attitude to the other and all others. In common life — whether the family, religious community, or any similar group — it is a fundamental law, identical for all. Mutual obedience is as valid for a husband and wife or brother and sister, as it is for the members of a religious community.

When a group has sufficiently strong structures and holds its unity by sharing diverse elements, it is clear that it requires an internal service of coordination and decision, without which it could not live and function. This is true both for a community and for a task-oriented group, even though the meaning of authority — for that is what is at question here — will not be the same in both cases. One must freely obey this authority since one accepts it as a service of unity. It goes without saying that the manner in which it is conceived and exercised depends on social and psychological conditions. In religious common life, authority serves the requirements of the gospel commitment in addition to those functions of order and coordination. But it does not differ that much from the authority exercised between a couple, or in a family, except that it is in no way paternal; religious communities are made of equal adults — all brothers and sisters.

Finally, in regard to work (professional life), each one must be allowed the greatest freedom of choice: each does what conforms to his taste and capacities. On the other hand, it must be recognized that, especially today, no one is absolutely free in the choice or exercise of his work. The constraints of life in society are, in fact, heavier and more burdensome each day. While choices remain possible, they are still rather limited.

To sum up, looking at the concrete reality of all human life, one sees that it is always lived between the two poles of freedom and submission. On the one hand, freedom, affirmation of oneself, initiative, responsibility, and, on the other side, listening to the other, the discovery and acceptance of limits which are imposed, and self-renunciation. Seen in this way, without myth, religious obedience, in its different applications, does not differ profoundly from the obedience which all men and women need to practice in accepting the constraints of human relations in the family or elsewhere, or in the requirements of home, professional, social, or political life. It is true that the motivations of obedience proposed to religious lean solidly on Scripture, which is not the usual case for the Christian living another vocation. But one should look closely to see whether there is an exaggeration here, or at least the application, in a secondary field, of texts which are primarily concerned with the reception of the gospel. Moreover, is it not ultimately true that the interdependence of one on the other, as well as to the inevitable structures, is in the end a demand of the gospel? Would not basing this interdependence more firmly on the gospel — even if we do not explicitly speak of obedience — render a great service to all Christians?

VI. CHASTITY

Religious are often described as those who have chosen and vowed perfect chastity. We hear it said that this religious and sacerdotal chastity is all the more necessary today since the world has been invaded by the erotic and needs clear testimony of mastery of self and respect for others. Who would not agree with this affirmation? Yet it leaves us somewhat uneasy. Are religious and celibate priests the only ones who can show the world the value of Christian chastity? What of other Christians, single and married? Are the demands of the gospel in this field any less for them?

To orient this discussion, it would be helpful to establish a certain number of distinctions at the start. What is proper to religious life is celibacy, i.e., the decision to live without committing oneself to the conjugal bond. This decision is founded on the gospel, which presents celibacy as a Christian possibility, and it is usually received and recognized publicly by the Church. Sacerdotal — priestly — celibacy, while it has the same content, is linked to a function: it is presently a prerequisite to performing the function. It cannot be forgotten that every unmarried man or woman is — need it be said — celibate. This is the situation for most human beings under the age of 25; and a large number even remain this way for their whole life.[24] Celibacy, rare as a definite state of life chosen for religious motives, is a common human reality for about half of the world population, if one regards it simply as the fact of being single and unmarried. This fact shows us already that one must not exaggerate when one presents celibacy as a rarity, almost abnormal or unnatural. Certainly, the celibacy of persons not yet married is open to the conjugal relation, and they remain available to it; in fact, it normally implies their search and pursuit. The celibacy of those who, past a certain age, have begun to assume their state as something definitive, is something else again. But, fundamentally, these situations have many points in common, especially in regard to a Christian concept of sexuality.

For chastity and continence, the point is the mastery, use, and orientation of sexuality and its genital forms according to human and Christian necessities. In the Christian ethical perspective, itself rooted in the Judaic tradition, genital sexual relations are reserved to the couple; apart from this they possess an incomplete or warped meaning.

Christian chastity is the true and meaningful use of genital sexuality, practiced in the life of the couple through bodily and spiritual love. This love, lived authentically in its depth, fidelity, and mutual respect, is — or at least could be — perfect chastity. Aside from the couple, chastity demands total continence of everyone, not only religious; although in the case of those not yet married it does not exclude the establishment of nor the search for the conjugal bond.

Things being so, we see that the fundamental demands of Christian chastity are identical for all. In presenting religious as the privileged — if not unique — testament of this chastity, do we not soften the radicalism of the Gospel on this point, which demands of all believers the same interior and exterior reserve? Would the behavior of an unmarried Christian seeking to live the gospel be any different from that of a religious as concerns chastity? Should not he or she be a witness — if need be, a resister — to an erotic world where pornography is displayed wholesale? Does not the married person fall under the same demand, beyond what is merely proper to him, to live a conjugal love intensely according to the truth of his body and his spirit?

Certainly, it can be said that religious — not the mass of Christians — have given and continue to give this witness. But is this not too often because they have been made specialists, leaving it understood that the others cannot in fact attain this level, or, worse yet, dare not by law attain it? Is the Gospel then valid only for a few?

VII. COMMUNITY

Except for hermits — who actually lived in groups most of the time — common (cenobitic) life has been a characteristic of religious life from its origins. Living together under the same roof, eating at the same table, holding everything in common, submitting themselves to a domestic order and to those responsible for it, seeking one and all the same ideal of Christian life (the teaching of the Word, prayer, Eucharist), the brothers and sisters believed they continued the form of the community in Jerusalem described in the Acts of the Apostles. This community — or fraternity — appeared to be the sign *par excellence* of the reconciliation made real by Christ, as well as the milieu where the fraternal love demanded by the gospel could be practiced.

This aspect is so obvious that it is almost useless to insist on it, only to say that this deep reality of the community — mutual love — has not always been presented as central; often, one saw only the useful side of the community, or its penitential aspect. The insistence on fraternity as a fundamental value is certainly one of the discoveries and the graces of our times. Never have we reflected so on the human and Biblical dimensions and demands of common life, never has the search been as wide as today to express this in new forms which are more true to those living it and more open to others. It is striking to note that it is not so much a theological system which is of interest, but a new human analysis. Above all, the horizontal dimension of this life is being discovered, as well as the structures and demands proper to it.

But at the same time that the concept and practice of religious life is being deepened for the greater good of the Church and the world, a current of considerable force is pushing all Christians to rediscover community. If love, to be true, must be exercised in a real, human environment, and if the Church is a community, it must be lived in an existential fashion, not only as a theoretical concept. Hence, a radical questioning of the current forms of Christian community. The latter, incarnate primarily in the forms of the traditional parish, appear totally inadequate. In fact, due first of all to numeric and geographic reasons, the Christian community of this type is an abstraction, not a reality. People are hardly known to one another, often not at all: it is impossible to speak of putting things in common, or of taking responsibility for one another. Sunday Eucharist is the only thing which assembles the members of a parish. This may be a call, a requirement of a reality to come (true community), but it is less and less an expressive sign of something already existing, for it is utterly meaningless to speak of communion between people who do not even know one another.

Thus we see small grassroot groups being born almost everywhere, which seek to create communities, not only abstract intentions. These groups listen to the word of God, celebrate the Eucharist, and perceive themselves as being in communion with all believers. They are in this way the Church; or at least have the intention of being so. But they want to create a true community of life: mutual knowledge, common concern for one another, sharing, the desire for common involvements — so many things which hardly existed in traditional parishes. This growing current, spreading under various names in many countries, signifies profound transformations. The Christian community is searching for an image, and this image will be one of sharing at all levels of life and activity. This movement, it can be seen, returns to what has been the fundamental project of all religious life: life in community. We see again that community itself is part of the Christian project as such. The attraction of certain monastic communities which really live a common life and the interest they sustain on the part of some lay groups are proof that the common life, even in its great diversity of forms, is at the heart of the Christian calling. Religious do not hold a monopoly; they simply live in an original way something to which all Christians are invited and which the Church tries unceasingly to create in the midst of a divided world.

CONCLUSIONS

The reader may be asking the point of these analyses. Without doubt, he has the impression that we wish to apply to all Christians what previously held only for religious. In other words, that we propose Gospel radicalism as a normal demand for all, as we explained in the different sections above.

Such, in fact, was the intention of the preceeding pages. If what has been set forth is accurate, the conclusion must be drawn that religious hold no monopoly on Christian life or its basic radicalism. This takes little from the religious, at most a pretension hardly in conformity with the Gospel and reality. But it proposes inexhaustible demands for everyone. If we can be accused of anything, it is that of being prone to rigorism or of dreaming of a Church of the pure and saintly. In fact, it is a matter of liberating these values — demythologizing them if need be — to make them available to all; for, all are called to live them from the moment they are caught up in the adventure of the Christian faith.

It is true that religious intend, from the start of their chosen vocation, to live faithfully according to the gospel, and this intention is clearly inscribed in the rules which inspire them. Let us also admit, since it corresponds to historical fact, that religious families have often responded better than the rest of the Christian community to the call of faith and that they have done so energetically and strikingly. Having done this, it is possible that they have also played a surrogate role, accomplishing as a particular group something which was and is the duty of all. But this does not mean that they hold exclusive rights. At most, at certain moments in the life of the Church, when the general level was declining, they had the grace and responsibility of maintaining in a living way what is at the heart of faith in Jesus.

If religious rules call men and women to radicalism and create structures which can express this, these rules are nothing but the call of the gospel. And this remains the fundamental — if not unique — rule of the community which is the Church. It is that which, in its entirety, in local as well as universal manifestations, is called living the whole gospel. Even knowing that a complete response will not be given, neither by a community nor by an individual, the demand remains the same; and it cannot be shifted to any group, not even a religious group.

Chapter IV

DEBATED QUESTIONS

There is no domain where religious life exists in tranquil possession of the truth: research and investigation are the rule everywhere. The preceeding pages demonstrated this in a general way, examining the fundamental significance of this life at the heart of the ordinary Christian vocation.

But, aside from this general problem, a certain number of points are the subject today of heated debate. I am thinking, for example, of celibacy — its Biblical foundations, its Christian and human meaning — and of the problems of lifelong commitment, historical continuity, the unity and diversity of religious life, and finally, the question of relations between the religious community and other groups (both Church and secular). In themselves these problems are secondary — they are the result of a certain concept of religious life which is itself the fundamental question. But they often sparked intense discussion, forcing themselves into relevancy.

In the following pages we will attempt to set these questions clearly in focus, indicating those directions which appear more sure than others. Our goal is not definitive theoretical answers, nor even practical solutions; we hope simply to shed new light on these questions which are in fact quite old, although they are raised with great urgency. Our approach will be more anthropological than theological. Too often, theological interpretations and syntheses are constructed before examining the evidence on its most basic, i.e. human, level. We thus proceed, bearing in mind the charge that Irenaeus of Lyon brought to the Gnostics, which concerns us as well: "Before becoming human, they seek to be like God."[25]

I. CONCERNING CELIBACY

Celibacy is only a small and secondary point among the various aspects of Christian existence. Considered along with faith or poverty, for example, which are basic demands of the life, it bears only relative importance; the temptation is to say it is of no importance. Along with and among other possibilities of living the unique call of the Gospel, it is but one possible response, no doubt significant.

We will avoid the question of priestly celibacy entirely, concentrating instead on the celibate religious. The former is of another order altogether, even though the content and meaning of Christian celibacy remain identical in both cases. Here, we believe, is the essential bond of religious life; celibacy is the principle, if not unique, element distinguishing this life from other forms of Christian living. For this reason, secondary as it may be, it merits attention and deserves reflection on its Christian sources and human meaning.

1. Biblical sources.

An historical question must be dealt with at the outset. If celibacy appeared and developed with Christianity, what happened before then? As we said above, it was really unknown to Biblical Judaism, and we can only speculate about groups like Qumran and the Essenes. We know that in Buddhism, monastic celibacy existed well before Christ. But, on the other hand, what meaning can we attribute to the celibacy of the vestal virgins or the corybantes, aberrant as it was? While we are inclined to affirm it, the question of the originality of Christian celibacy must remain open.

In fact, the question is raised in chapter seven of the first letter of Paul to the Corinthians (under what influence, Christian or otherwise?). With no clear directive from the Lord on this subject, Paul reckons by virtue of his apostolic charism that the situation of the Christian living in celibacy has a positive meaning: it is a possibility offered to believers, and it is good, especially if given eschatological urgency. We leave the matter here, having written more completely on the subject elsewhere. On the level of apostolic tradition — constitutive and normative for the Church — celibacy is presented as a Christian vocation. It is not seen as a "counsel of perfection" in the meaning later attributed to the term, but as a free possibility holding certain advantages. This seems more than sufficient as a Biblical foundation.

Taking the next step, can we assert that we have here a wish or a word of Christ himself? Not that the counsel of Paul is less certain or without value, since we accept the teaching of the Apostles as a foundation of our faith. But we find in Matthew (19, 10-12) a *logia* of the Lord, usually interpreted as alluding to celibacy. The interpretation of this passage (concerning those who become eunuchs for the sake of the kingdom of God) has recently been challenged.[26] The point is not that men decide to live in celibacy (as eunuchs) for the sake of the kingdom, but that married men who have been abandoned by their wives should not remarry since the demands of Christ forbid divorce and remarriage.

This is obviously a question of exegesis. The short pericope on the eunuchs found only in Matthew (although the parallel passage on divorce appears in Mark) may be a part of a total narrative unknown to Mark in this state, or Mark could simply have omitted this part. Or is it an independent *logia* appended to another theme under Matthew's redaction, as was his style? The meaning of the text is different under each of these possibilities. If the two parts (divorce and eunuchs) were originally linked, then the second must undeniably be viewed in light of the first. On the other hand, the *logia* taken by itself clearly concerns celibacy.

Most exegetes, old and new, have leaned toward the second possibility. Dom Dupont, while opting for the first, concludes that the text also concerns the situation of the celibates (as a matter of consequence), which forces the text somewhat, in our opinion. If the text is in fact a reference to abandoned husbands, it can have nothing to do with celibacy, except through a deduction little related to exegesis.

We believe that the arguments of Dupont and Quesnell come nowhere near settling the exegetical question of the meaning of this *logia* on the eunuchs. The common interpretation of this pericope seems more justified; not because without it there would be no Scriptural foundation for celibacy (at any rate, we have the text mentioned above in Paul, and we do not need the *ipsissima verba Christi* for everything), but simply for exegetical reasons.

We have outlined the basis for a longer study on celibacy, and we welcome such an effort. But at the current state of exegetical research, the fact remains that celibacy is something real in the New Testament. It would be false to claim that it is without Scriptural sources, even if it develops that the *logia* of Matthew 19, 12 bears no relation to it.

2. Meaning.

While the possibility of celibacy as a Christian vocation appears well established, the situation is less clear regarding its meaning. The latter has been well studied — overly much, perhaps — along spiritual and mystical lines, and not nearly enough in terms of human, psychological, and social dimensions, etc.

The Biblical texts cited above provide almost no leads here. While the text from Matthew concerns celibacy, in our opinion, it simply affirms that such a choice is possible by virtue of a decision of faith: "for the sake of the Kingdom." But nothing is said of the inner meaning of such a step.

The passage from 1 Corinthians which speaks of celibacy is situated in a marked eschatological context. The present world is passing away and, with it, all its constitutive structures, of which marriage is one example. Also, to avoid "the tribulations of the flesh" linked to the disappearance of these structures, and to be oriented wholly toward what is coming, it is better not to marry. Whoever is married becomes tied, in any case, to something which will no longer exist in the coming age. We have here, first of all, an affirmation that marriage is an institution of the current world, destined to disappear. Secondly, it is preferable to remain celibate for the sake of harmony with the new situation which will be inaugurated. In this text there is a certain affinity with the word of the Lord reported by the Synoptics (Mt. 22, 30 and parallels), according to which the situation of those resurrected is of another sort entirely, especially regarding relations between the sexes. In the Pauline view, Christian celibacy is thus an anticipation of the life to come; this, because its opposite, marriage, is a provisional element, destined to disappear. It seems difficult for us to draw more from this on the level of internal meaning.

We must add that Paul speaks as well of an undivided attachment to the Lord (7, 32-35) which celibacy provides for the unmarried man. We believe that this motivation should not be understood from a moral perspective — as if loving one's husband or wife were to detract something from the love given to God and be therefore "divisive" — but eschatologically, in the meaning indicated above, since marriage inserts men and women into the provisional, in the tension between what is and what is to come.

What is true is that from this text on the non-divided man and his undivided attachment to the Lord, understood in a moral sense, a theological interpretation of celibacy was developed little by little. Following this interpretation, celibacy (virginity) gives men and women greater freedom, a particular availability to grow closer to God and to Christ. The relationship of a celibate man or woman to God is different from that of someone married: it is easier, at least in itself, to reach a more profound intimacy, a more encompassing love. In sum, celibacy chosen for the sake of the kingdom would have an essentially vertical dimension: it establishes man in a special relationship with God.

This line of interpretation (bride of Christ, greater love for God, availability for prayer, etc.) can claim a tradition so old (*Method of Olympus* of the third century) that it is current even today and has tenacious roots. It raises serious questions, however. It presupposes that conjugal love, in itself, competes with love of God. One involved in this bond, so it goes, is placed in a more ambiguous, or less straightforward, relationship with God and Christ than one unmarried. After careful consideration, however, we can see why such presuppositions are unacceptable. The bond between a couple is essentially (or at least ideally) an interpersonal relation of mutual acceptance and responsibility — in a word, a bond of love. In itself it does not differ fundamentally, except perhaps in its depth and intimacy, from all truly interpersonal bonds. All men and women are called by their very being to establish these bonds, for without them they would be unable to exist. And if we want to reserve the name love for the conjugal bond, we call these interpersonal relations friendship, fraternity, etc. The gospel command to love one another constantly reminds us of the prime value of these bonds for the scope of Christian living.

If this is true, that without love of neighbor there is no love of God, one can ask why conjugal love should itself be an obstacle to the love of God. Because it can be egotistical, closed on itself? But all human relations face the same danger. Because it is linked to sexuality? But this is true as well for all relations, since sexuality is the necessary dimension for all desire of the other. Or because it is linked, more exactly, to genital sexuality? Admittedly, sexuality in general, as well as in its genital expressions, is ambiguous, but no more or less so than other human dynamisms or instincts (the will to power, aggressiveness, etc.). To think that genital sexuality in itself raises a kind of murky veil between God and man is to succumb to a dualistic conception of man, to a magical view of what is unclean and pure, sacred and profane. Exterior things do not render man impure, but what can separate him from God and defile him are those things in his heart, at the center of his person. Thus, it seems that the meaning of celibacy is not to be sought on the vertical plane (relations between man and God) but on the horizontal (what can change in our relations with one another). For in the relation between man and God we all stand before the same mystery, at once near and inaccessible, whether married or not; and there is no human relation, aside from something unhealthy to begin with (true as well on the human level itself) which can place us differently.

Now to be precise, there have been many theological explanations of celibacy, the majority of which in our opinion are still in great need of discussion and clarification; but not until recently has there been much that pauses to touch on its human dimensions.[27] Much certainly has been said and written about chastity, even to the point of obsession; it has been examined from the point of view of all men, all Christians, and according to the vocation of each. As for celibacy, we have spoken of the mystical marriage, of the love of Christ, of freedom to pray and serve God, but hardly anyone has questioned the significance of being celibate in psychological or social terms. But this is a fundamental notion.

It is not a matter of pursuing an analysis which requires particular competence or study, but of asking some questions which can lead, as we have said, to fruitful lines of research.

The first question relates to celibacy in its specific nature, as remaining unmarried becomes a choice and state of life. As such, celibacy is first of all a relational solitude (the exclusion of the bond of love between men and women) and, consequently, sexual solitude. But to say solitude is not necessarily to affirm something negative. Solitude is also a value where a person finds and affirms himself and deepens his interior life. In this regard, celibacy offers advantages which the married person, linked to a family, would have difficulty finding. Solitude is also a void, an absence. The celibate must accept this negative side, that is to say, the impossibility of forming a relation which, if successful, could be one of the greatest values of human life.

Nevertheless, celibacy is not simply a negation: excluding one relational possibility, it opens the door to all the others, placing a vital dynamism at their service. Further reflection is necessary here, starting with facts and experiences, on the relational universe of the celibate, on the possibility and importance of friendships in his or her life, and on the community as the most apt setting for actualizing relationships. These are basic directions, for it appears that the success of celibacy is linked to this dimension. Everything else — freedom for service, for work, for different kinds of commitments (scientific, political, etc.) — depends on the positive use of this first freedom: the freedom to enter into deep and numerous relationships.

It is against this background of relational fulfillment that we can view the meaning of celibacy; it is here that we must study questions concerning the sexual (or genital) life of the celibate. As we have said, the demands of a total internal and external continence are no different for the celibate than for all other unmarried Christians. Mastery of self, of one's imagination and fantasies, honesty and transparency in one's relations with others, both men and women — these are the objectives which must be progressively sought and attained. This necessitates self-knowledge, an understanding of one's dynamisms and complexes, lucidity and realism without any puritanism, but also without compromise.

Since one's ability to form relationships is the fundamental necessity, it should also serve as the criterion for determining an aptitude for celibacy. The best preparation for celibacy is no different from that necessary for marriage. In principle, an unsuccessful celibate would not make a good husband, nor a bad husband a good celibate.

Reading these reflections, one might perhaps see a kind of total horizontalism. Can we still speak of evangelical celibacy if the meaning of celibacy is found exclusively on the plane of human relations or if we say that man's relationship to God is in no way modified by it? Are we functioning on a purely humanistic level, no more or no less, or even on the level of illusion? We believe that if celibacy can be recognized on the level of its meaning as a valid human option with its own self-contained rationale (and we do have evidence, admittedly rare, that celibacy does successfully exist totally aside from religious motivation), then on the level of decision — or motivation — celibacy can also be a Christian choice. Because celibacy is presented as a choice for the sake of the kingdom, and in the light of the present eschatological reality, Christians are able to make this choice as an act of faith and confidence. Such a decision is not a blind leap of faith, since we know that celibacy has its own inner meaning on the strictly human level. It is nevertheless an act of faith, since it is done by virtue of the call and promise of Christ and in the vision of the new world which is to come.

A celibacy thus embraced and lived — in spite of the limits and weaknesses inherent in all human reality — is a sign with multiple meanings. It affirms the mastery of man over the merely biological, in order to emphasize non-genital relationships. The greater part of human relations, in fact, occur on this level, and the celibate shows that the absence of genital bonds is not destructive of men and women. A celibacy which finds its fulfillment in relationships and friendships within a group of the same sex shows, moreover, that relationships based on sexual differentiation are not the absolute model of all true and deep interpersonal encounter. Through this sociological non-conformity (the fact of remaining single in a society where the family is the dominant social model) another freedom of men and women is manifested as well: the freedom to refuse to accept certain structures otherwise considered fundamental. Perhaps the celibate is pointing the way to a future state of the human race and its structure of relationships; to the day when it will pass beyond genital sexuality.

If this seems a utopian dream in evolutionary terms, we at least believe that celibacy is a sign foreshadowing the world of the resurrection where all human relations, especially physiological bonds, will be radically transfigured. In this sense, celibacy has an eschatological dimension for faith, for it points toward what will be, toward the day when there will no longer be man nor woman, but when all will be "sons of the resurrection" (Lk. 20, 36).

II. LIFELONG COMMITMENT

Even before the emergence of the cenobitic life, virgins and domestic ascetics committed themselves before the Church to living in celibacy and continence. Basil was familiar with this commitment to virginity; one has the impression, however, that for him the idea of commitment to common gospel life coincided with the baptismal commitment.[28] In the Benedictine Rule, this commitment is described with some precision, and infidelity is considered a sin against God. In fact, whatever form it has taken (*professio, promissio, receptio ad obedientiam, votum*), religious life supposed or explicitly required a definite commitment to live in such a way.

Today, in a world more sensitive to change than to continuity or permanence, the question is whether or not a definite religious commitment is possible at all. This question, in turn, raises another, even more fundamental: can a man or woman make a lifelong commitment? One can see that this is less a theological problem than a question about man himself. It is along these lines that we will pursue our reflection.

1. The meaning of commitment.

When we speak of commitment, we think of someone shaping a project for himself. This project to do or to accomplish something finds its extension in time, otherwise it would be immediately realized. Man desires to bring his project to fruition, to remain faithful to it; he knows that it holds a valuable and significant direction for him. But time, mysteriously unfolding in its unknowable duration, always steps in. One never knows what it holds for him, either in terms of external factors, or especially at the heart of one's own self, when making a decision today. Commitment, then, is an affirmation of the permanence of a decision, of the will to hold to it, to remain faithful, whether for a time or, in certain cases, for always. Thus, in committing himself man considers what he wants to do, his orientation, the choice which he has already made and the projects he has shaped; and, projecting himself into the future, he affirms himself as in control over the duration of time, as capable of maintaining his present decision and realizing it in the future. Commitment appears to be a kind of mastery and victory of man over time.

The decision of which we speak and by which man achieves his victory over the passing of time is accomplished, to be sure, in the interior of his conscience. It is not a single act, but a continuing effort to grapple with passing time. Each day, one's fidelity is reaffirmed and one's orientation corrected by virtue of the initial project. Usually this decision concerns others as well: that is why it will often take on a certain solemnity, at least at the initial moment. Man gives his word, commits himself, binds himself by contract, and does so before witnesses representing a group, a society. This presence, these public witnesses are a guarantee and support for him, especially when the decision concerns them.

It is necessary to recall that human life, especially in its social dimension, rests on the commitments of one to the others. Man should be able to count on others, on their presence, work, and fidelity to assure a certain order. He does count on them in this way and in most cases it is because he believes that the others will be faithful to what they have promised to do, to their commitments. This is also true of man considered in himself: the man who remains faithful to a project that he considers essentially his own is seen as someone on whom others can rely.

Let us apply this analysis to religious commitment. There, it is also a matter of a project, that of living a certain type of Christian existence: radical evangelism, celibacy, and community of brothers and sisters. Having come to know that this kind of life has a meaning for me, that it is a way for me to live fully my vocation as a human and as a Christian, and having been accepted by those who already form this community, I am able to commit myself to living this way both today and in the future.

All the more so, since such a commitment coincides essentially with an act of Christian faith. By this I understand that I am giving my life a definite meaning, and that I will hold to this line of development through all the fluctuations of both time and my own will.

Religious commitment concerns myself first of all, for "holding to one's word means to make an effort to maintain a certain meaning of oneself, once one has recognized that this meaning is constitutive of personal existence."[29] It means that I build myself; I am not at the whim of exterior and interior upheavals, but am able to imprint a certain continuity on all that I become.

But this commitment concerns others at the same time, especially the community within which I hope to realize my life project. I integrate myself into this human group, I bind myself to it in order to participate in a common creation, where each will be created by the other. Moreover, this is a two-sided commitment; for, while I commit myself to living with my brothers following the same fundamental direction, they are committed as a group to offering me this possibility, to receiving me as a totally active member. Thus, my commitment is not a purely internal decision but a kind of contract, somewhat akin to marriage: not, certainly, with God but with the community. There lies its public and solemn character, since it is made before the community, using a symbolic ritual. Again, for this reason and since it is entered into communally at about the same age as a marriage commitment, there are certain traits of resemblance between the two; all the more so, since it carries with it the specific object of life in celibacy. As we have seen, the latter has reference to the fundamental relational scope of life, the same as marriage.

Religious commitment is expressed before the community, or at least before its representatives: in fact, before the Church which the community represents. This presence is not only that of a witness, but of a partner; there is a reception, an insertion into the group. Thus the commitment is bilateral: mutual giving and receiving. It is made likewise before God, not God considered as a partner, but as a witness or guarantee. Commitment before God presupposes that one comes before him as one is, with one's weakness and instability, but with one's life project and will to continuity as well. It is this leaning on God which gives man meaning and value, and brings the believer the ability to affirm a project for the future and remain faithful to it.

2. Commitment for life.

It is relatively easy to admit the necessity of certain commitments; without them the life of men and women would be impossible. One must, in fact, be able to rely on others, on their fidelity and on the permanence of their decisions. But one question raised today concerns the possibility of a lifelong commitment. Can man set an orientation for himself and commit himself irrevocably to it without illusion and presumption?

Let us say first of all that such commitments remain exceptional. Aside from rather vague commitments to patriotism or a service, for example, we are almost always dealing with commitments among persons. The most clear and frequent examples are marriage and religious profession. Curiously once again, these two cases resemble one another on certain points. Religious profession inasmuch as it is a commitment to gospel life does not differ from the act of faith and permanent fidelity required of all Christians. What is original is the commitment to live in a community, and this on the basis of celibacy. As we mentioned previously, such a choice is in general made in the same period of life in both categories, married and nonmarried. Man then sees himself definitely inserted into the structures of life according to the option he has chosen, marriage or celibacy.

If we understand that a life commitment can only be made on the fundamental choices, and that it remains rare, the question nevertheless remains: is it reasonable? Is it possible?

Our response is in line with the direction already initiated in this reflection. Can man desire to give a definitive orientation to his life? Can he set a project for himself, with the understanding

that he will not deviate from its demands? If the answer is yes —
and we think it is, since it seems to us that the dignity and value
of man lies precisely in this permanent creation of self in time
according to a chosen meaning — then lifelong commitment is
possible. It means that man believes in his own continuity, he
considers himself capable of building it freely, without becoming
the plaything of outside influences. To believe in the validity of
a lifelong commitment is to have faith in one's will and one's
freedom, as a dynamism which creates and dominates the passing
of time.

One can add that on a sociological level, lifelong commitment
seems indispensable for the building of community. We cannot
create something together unless we are committed to being
together, especially when the object is not so much a task to be
accomplished as the development of a common life. Otherwise,
there is uncertainty and instability; everything becomes problema-
tical. And this is unhealthy when the question is as serious as
the choice of celibacy.

Finally, since we are concerned ultimately with a faith decision,
we stand under the same demands as anyone committed to
Christian life with its imperatives: a commitment is made once
and for all, yet at the same time one tries to be faithful each day,
aware that this fidelity is not a permanent possession, but something which is created at every instant.

3. Different kinds of commitments.

If we have insisted on the viability of lifelong commitment, it
is because it seems fundamental for the meaning of man and
common creation and, on the other hand, because it is precisely
what is being questioned today. We think that without it no
attempt at common life can hold, and that the person becomes
an easy prey for all sorts of fluctuations. "And to drift is not to be
free, it is to be a prisoner of all the breaking waves" (Karl Barth).

Nevertheless, one can envisage different possibilities in the
concrete. As soon as there is a permanent and stable core, one can

conceive of a certain number of persons gathering around that center to live the same life, but for a time, without a particular commitment. Normally, one should be clear about the length of time one proposes to live in this way, however. Otherwise, no project, no enterprise is possible. At any rate, this will not happen without problems.

The concept of temporary commitment presents another possibility: it has been a practice, in fact, for several centuries of religious life. It has a meaning for the one who is unable to make a lifelong commitment but who still seeks a certain stability for himself and for his community. But is such a commitment really an ideal, especially if it is prolonged and repeated? Either it is based on a definitive project — and why rely on temporary forms if this is so? — or it expresses hesitation and uncertainty, which in spite of the idea of commitment is based on indecision, harmful for both the individual and the group. As for the practice of temporary commitments before a definitive commitment, it seems to lack meaning. On the one hand, one devalues the very idea and seriousness of commitment by repetition and the frequent ease of dispensation. On the other hand, this supposes a debatable concept of vow and its meritorious character. The simplest attitude is to wait for the moment, for both the individual and the community, when the commitment will have its full meaning. This time, which should not be too long — one does not wait indefinitely before deciding — should be concluded by one definite and decisive act. Moreover, practically speaking, we know well that a person who decides to join a community and who enters to prepare himself for a lifelong commitment is already interiorly committed by the fact of his project and his intention. His first reception into the community, ordinarily marked by a symbolic gesture, is in itself the first public commitment.

Until now we have used the term "commitment" almost exclusively; the fact is that it has been rare in religious vocabulary. The object was to demythologize a certain number of themes attached to the word "vow" through an especially anthropological reflection, and to rediscover the fundamental element marking the insertion of a person into a community of gospel living.

What appears essential to us is the act of giving one's word, one's promise to affirm a project of life which one wants to make definite for oneself, doing so before one's brothers and sisters, before the Church and before God. We call this decision, which has always taken on a public character and a symbolic (ritual) aspect, profession. The legal forms and moral interpretations given to it throughout the centuries are secondary, particularly the concept of vow in the vocabulary and in practice, which became current only later (the Middle Ages). To call this profession or lifelong commitment a vow, promise, or oath is a casuistic and legal subtlety. What is important is the intention of a person expressed solemnly and publicly: from this comes its greatness and power to commit.

It thus seems important to free the notion of commitment (or profession) from its often-complicated legal trappings (solemn vows, simple vows, temporary vows, etc.). Not to diminish it, but to put value on what constitutes its greatness.

III. HISTORICAL CONTINUITY

We saw in Chapter II that nearly all of religious life existing today is bound to the past, either near or distant. Aside from two or three recent developments, we must speak of groups inserted in an historical continuity through their reference to their origins, their rule and their tradition, which are often quite ancient. The forms open to a Christian considering commitment to religious life all carry a history, a defined spiritual tradition and structures inherited from the past. This person is faced with the reality of entering into an already-existing dynamism (or heavily weighted structure as is oftentimes the case) than of creating something new. Such are the hard facts.

In the face of this fact, two contradictory currents emerge: a return to the sources and a rejection of the past.

By the mere fact that a particular group exists, we can assume its

past intention to continue its original experience, repeatedly re-
ferring to this experience as a criterion of its fidelity. Today, too,
the efforts at renewal currently engaged in by all religious families are based on a return to the sources and on fidelity to the
spirit of their founders. Contemporary methods of investigation
allow a more exact knowledge of the past; moreover, historical
studies have multiplied and their conclusions, often bearing directly on concrete living, are placed at the disposition of all.

If the multiplication of these historical studies is cause for
rejoicing, it is paralleled, especially among young people, with
a general contestation of the past. Historical meaning and reference to the past are not the strong points of today's mentality.
Many believe that the answers to contemporary questions and
research are not found by looking backward, but to the present
or even the future. This lack of interest rests on the attitude that
it is difficult to see the meaning of the past for today. On the
level of religious life, this means that the past, ignored more and
more, is unable to be seen as a source of inspiration for life today.
From this results the abandonment of study and reflection. If
there is to be a return, it is to the gospel, not to traditions, especially to the latter in their most recent forms. Religious life
must be created anew today, all the more so since the forms which
are held as depositories of tradition are often unadapted and
oriented toward what no longer exists.

The necessity and limits of tradition.

What is the proper attitude toward these contradictory orientations? Must we truly break with the past, entering into a sort of
permanent creation "ex nihilo," or does continuity still have a
value today? And what value?

Let us start with the facts. What is immediately obvious is that
religious life is situated in very precise continuities: reference
to a particular rule, to a particular charismatic figure, to a particular experience. New forms certainly exist today, but even
they already have a history, even if it is one of only twenty-five

years. There are also many small groups which appear, here and there, without any links to the past; one can well believe their search and widespread growth is full of promise. But one should also realize, however one may regard this sprouting up, that most of these experiences are ephemeral. For, one needs a very particular charism to create something new, and although the Spirit may not be stingy today, it is somewhat presumptuous to imagine that one possesses it automatically from the moment one decides to create something new. At any rate, reference to the past is not absent in the serious and authentic cases, since one always profits from the experiences of others.

One fact looms large: religious life today comes to us in forms tied to the past. Entering them, one should assume this historical dimension. Whatever their deplorable cumbersomeness and inflexibility, what strikes the impartial observer in most cases is their dynamism and the very youth of these traditions. Does it not witness to the power of the original inspiration and permanence of their dynamism that men of the twentieth century are interested in a rule of the sixth (Benedict) or that in 1970 nearly 50,000 men claim to hold to the experience of Francis of Assisi, finding there a reason for their way of living? The charism given once to a man remains meaningful centuries afterwards: this is a victory over time, a manifestation of the communion of saints through the years. It is also a reminder, at a time when man is losing his historical roots, of the value of continuity. We cannot grow as persons or as Christians without seeing ourselves on a line which joins the present to the past to create the future. For the Christian this means that the gospel cannot be lived except in a communion which embraces not only the present but also the past. If it is true that the gospel must constantly be rediscovered in its newness, it is no less true that it reaches us by a sort of horizontal line running from the Resurrection to the return of Christ. We create neither the gospel nor life according to it: we submit ourselves to both; for, one and the other exist at the heart of the living community. This community is not a purely abstract

event, but an often weighty reality which is nevertheless important because it carries life. For a Christian seeking the particular
type of commitment that is religious life, it is a historical community which offers it to him.

But how can we master and exploit this historical dimension
which, as we have seen, can also block and prevent life? At
the beginning, a historical step is necessary. We come to a
knowledge which unfolds the essential lines of an experience and
an historical text. While specialists have a particular role to play
in research, the results, at least in their fundamentals, should be
known to all those interested in this tradition. Next comes the
step of interpretation. Here we separate the essential from the
secondary points. It is important also to grasp the relationship between what emerges as fundamental and permanent and as a simple
historical conditioning. But the historical step is not everything.
A certain meaning, a spiritual discernment linked to the experience one lives in continuity will allow one to distinguish what
remains valuable as an ever-present dynamism. Ultimately, it is
difficult to identify intellectually what constitutes continuity: in
addition to being a necessary theoretical element, it is a matter
of spiritual intuition.

It is not a question, either, of restricting oneself to reproduc-
tion or literal mimicry: what remains is a dynamism that is
oriented toward a certain direction or toward a certain viewpoint pointing to the gospel. Starting from this, the space is wide
open for a new creation, for a contemporary way of moving for-
ward on the same path. The ideal is not to repeat what has been
done by the prototype, but to create something anew by virtue of
the same momentum. This is exciting, but demanding as well. So,
even in the midst of continuity, there is the possibility for permanent creation.

Is this to say that all historical traditions have a future? Let
us say that, whatever else they can claim, none of these traditions has been given the promise of eternity! While we can believe that religious life as such forms an integral part of the life

of the Church, we are unable to affirm that all its historical forms — even one or two of them — will stand the test of time. Except for very rare cases, history proves the contrary. It seems to us that the closer an experience or text is to the gospel, transmitting only its essentials, then it is the more original, flexible, and linked to a truly powerful historical figure. At the same time, it is less conditioned sociologically and more open to the future. For, then it is presented as a charismatic crystalization of gospel demands, a practical demonstration of its possibilities. Its call preserves an astonishing power of attraction through the centuries. Is this the case for all traditions? To think so would be an illusion. The current crisis of religious life will serve to reveal this: it will affirm what is valuable and eliminate what has seen its time. But in this last case, what solution can we foresee for those traditions condemned to disappear which still claim the commitments of many men and women? There is certainly the possibility of re-organization or affiliation with the living families or, even better, an effort to reach beyond the unhappy expressions at the heart of these enterprises in the past, that is, to create a possibility for gospel life. Then this will be a new beginning.

As for those who believe they must live inside those traditions which are renewing themselves and where there seems to be a vigorous dynamism at work, they must weigh their responsibilities, not only toward the heritage they must hold in value for the good of all, but also toward those who have recently joined them. To refuse to pass on a continuity would be resignation and a lack of fidelity. It would also be presumption, for the charism of the beginnings is not given to all.

We believe that the times now are a blessing for religious life. For, it has known self-renewal, choosing the correct path so many times in the course of centuries, and we know it will not lack this understanding today. Because the change that we are living is deep and the death of the past is painful to many, it is permissible to think that the renaissance will be magnificent.

IV. THE UNITY AND DIVERSITY OF RELIGIOUS LIFE

Since the Middle Ages, religious life in the West has assumed a great diversity of forms and denominations. To the monks and canons regular have been added the mendicants, among whom the diversity is even greater. Since the sixteenth century groups have multiplied and can be counted in scores on the men's side and in hundreds on the women's. Each of these groups, where the numeric importance might vary between tens of thousands and dozens of members, is independent, is called by a particular name, possesses its own proper laws, and believes itself the repository of an original charism useful, if not necessary, to the life of the Church. Moreover, at the very heart of identical spiritual traditions (monasticism, the Franciscan family, Carmelites, etc.) there are further splits which are perhaps historically explainable but difficult to justify today. To an outside observer all this seems strange: it seems a dispersion, a waste of spiritual energy; people make the effort to justify and keep alive these particularities having no importance.

And the question comes up: should these differences be maintained and even accentuated, should an identity be sought within these close frames of reference without regard for the others, or should they be abandoned to form a single type of general religious life which is not differentiated? In the face of the current crisis, do not particularities lose their meaning in the rush of events?

For us, the solution is not to be found in the extremes: neither in a closed and musty particularity, nor in a depersonalizing and impoverishing leveling. It would be appropriate to favor a movement toward communion which would lead to unity in the long run through the fusion of a certain number of religious families and which would safeguard the diversity of gifts which is the heritage of religious life while bringing them out of isolation.

1. From isolation to communion.

First of all, coming out of isolation. In spite of contacts "at the top" (between major superiors in Rome and at the national level) and greater communication between groups, there is still some distance to travel. Although general theological reflection on religious life is being made in common and to the profit of everyone, when it comes to the specific charism of each group everything has been fairly hidden until now. A group seeks to define itself without taking others into account or, often, by identifying itself with an image the others would reject. Thus monasticism — a form of religious life which refers to an ancient tradition (the fourth to sixth centuries) — defines itself exclusively by reference to the traditions of this epoch. The question seems definitely settled as far as the forms of religious life which appear later are concerned: they are viewed as something of another nature entirely, as specialized or functional groups. But there are still groups appearing after these centuries which cannot be classified in these categories: these groups (e.g., those of Franciscan or Carmelite tradition) are considered as having no function save the living of a certain type of life according to the Gospel.

Going even further, when the "mendicants" reacted against "monastic" traits in their life believing that these traits weighed down their own tradition, it is important to note that certain monks would refuse, in the name of historical truth, to consider these traits as legitimate monastic tradition. At the most, they might be considered medieval. While a given group might in fact know its own spiritual tradition well enough most of the time, comparisons with other traditions usually err through ignorance. Whether we wish it or not, we never define ourselves against an absolute, but as being similar or complementary to others, especially when it comes to originality at the heart of the same vocation. The same is true in the process of personal identification: through contact, by meeting and confronting others, we come to know ourselves in our originality. It is often worse. Spiritual families with the same origins but now divided into distinct groups (Benedictines and Cistercians, Franciscans and Capuchins, Carmelites and Discalced Carmelites), while maintaining official contacts and even pursuing common projects on a grassroot level, all pursue separate reflection and a separate *aggiornamento* by themselves, without even inviting "observers" from the other branch to their chapters of renewal, although they ask the same questions and often develop the same answers. This is indeed an incomprehensible anomaly. Decidedly, ecumenism is less advanced here than among separated churches!

It seems as if the time has come to reflect on our originality with, and in the presence of, others; we are thus freed of myths and false opposition, and the charism of each, when it exists, will emerge on its own. The criticism and questioning of others is always a gain. We emerge from it more truly and clearly ourselves. For, we are able to note a deep common identity: there is only one and the same fundamental religious life. The essential differences are marked by the two major currents: religious life in itself (life according to a certain evangelical line) and "functional" religious life (with one or more concrete tasks to perform). The particularities within each current are not such that they require a separate type of religious life each time. There will be charisms, different emphases, relative nuances.

It is possible that such confrontations will lead many groups, especially the smaller ones, to unions or fusions, their great resemblances and minor differences being seen for what they are. For everyone it will mean greater knowledge of the others, a feeling of great unity and respect for irreducible and complementary charisms. For, the different forms of religious life must be lived in reciprocity.

2. Diversity of gifts.

While criticizing isolation and the artificial opposition it harbors and while welcoming and predicting regroupings and fusions in the future, we must take care not to reduce religious life to a single, unique form. This would be a view of the spirit which fails to take into account the existing variety and complexity.

It is historically undeniable that spiritually diverse traditions and sensibilities have existed and have found their own original expressions in the religious families. It suffices to enumerate a few of these families to see what is unique about them. The ancient tradition of monasticism, even with its past and present variations, is not reducible in spite of whatever affinities (often ignored) it has with the Franciscan movement. Dominicans and Jesuits are not different solely on account of their different names and origins; the Carmelites and the Little Brothers of Jesus, both "contemplatives," share neither the same references nor spiritual approach.

It is not for us to define the origin of each group; this may be an impossible task. While it is true that in each case living the totality of the Christian message is of fundamental import, it is likewise true that each has an original approach, building an intuitive synthesis from one particular point and not another. It is difficult intellectually to designate the particular characteristic of each, but it exists and is manifested by a different sensibility and different reaction. There is no need to draw hard and fast lines, but the fact remains that a certain monastic (or Franciscan, or Jesuit) type exists. Each type not only reads the Gospel and sees man in an original way, it has its own historical heritage and spirit. Unfortunately, history has shown us too often that the dangers of isolation, particularism, and even chauvinism exist.

And yet the oft-heard idea of a regrouping or general fusion of all religious life seems not only utopian but dangerous, even mortally so, for this life. Must we rush from the one extreme of dispersion to a new monolith, a general leveling, impersonalism? In an age where each person and each group seeks their own originality and where a strong movement towards decentralization and regionalism can be felt, must we level religious life to create a kind of uniform army? Does such a thing as abstract religious life exist? Has it ever existed? Has not the life of a group always been formed around one man or woman or movement? The artificial creation by administrative decree of a forced unity would be a blow directed at the heart of religious life, which is itself precisely a protest against such general leveling of frameworks and institutions. The person committing himself to religious life is not inserted into an abstraction, but into a world of living men and women, into a current running through history with traditions, structures — in a word, into a concrete community.

What way can we foresee then to avoid isolation and particularism without falling into a leveling down? We should take our inspiration from Orthodox monasticism. The latter has known how to preserve its fundamental unity: there is one monasticism, one profession. But each monastery or each group, in communion with the local bishop, has the freedom to draw its inspiration from a particular rule, or even to introduce another. In effect, the East (like the West before the Carolingian era) knows no obligation to group around a unique rule: all the rules — of Basil, Pachomius, etc. — are considered spiritual texts and are equally consulted, without making them juridical documents.[30] Certainly, the situation in the West is so different and the ways of doing things so contrary there that it would be an illusion to attempt to copy the East. We can nevertheless imagine a single profession (along the line of that being suggested by the new ritual), a single name (monk or religious), a similar vestment to be worn for worship and official occasions, a greater possibility for moving from one group to the other and, finally, fusion for those groups having affinities.

It is important to be aware of the facts in each situation and to join in the movement towards unity respecting the diversity of each. The current crisis in which all are equally challenged, the shuffling of ideas and experiences — in a word, life itself — will do the rest.

V. RELIGIOUS LIFESTYLE: SEPARATE OR DIFFUSE

From its origins until today, the lifestyle of religious has always appeared different from that of other Christians. The chosen lifestyle of religious placed them on the margins of ordinary society, making them something "separate." This separation was more or less emphasized in respective periods. At great moments — the time of the monastic origins or the Franciscan movement, for example — while there were ruptures demanded by the kind of life being chosen, there was no search for artificial separation. Thus the first Friars Minor worked like and with other men, dressed more or less like the poor of their time and lived in roadside shelters and shacks. However, with the aid of a certain conservatism, structures fostering separation were quickly created.

As we mentioned in the first chapter above, religious life today still comprises a world apart with regard to houses, domestic order, work, and contacts. This is changing very rapidly; most barriers (habits, cloister, convents, kinds of work) have already disappeared or are on the way out. The life style, especially in small groups, has become practically secular, which is to say, resembling that of the family. There are no more front parlors: people are received into one's home to share the same life, the same table, and often the same prayer.

The question then arises: just how far can we widen the framework of this life? Does it not demand a distinct and separate reality with its own identity? Or should it be broken open, "liberated," made open and accessible to all? In other words, would it not be appropriate, while maintaining celibacy and community life, to join with celibates of the other sex, with couples, even with older members of the group who have since married? Is it even possible to conceive of a lifestyle — community of goods, prayer, etc. — in which one could move from celibacy to marriage without changing one's vocation? These are not hypothetical questions: there are religious groups where they are effectively raised. All this implies on the one hand a desire to open to other Christians the possibility of communal gospel life and, moreover, to become enriched through their presence and questioning. On the other hand, there also seems to be uncertainty about the value of a definitive lifelong commitment, especially relating to celibacy. Serious research on unprecedented and possible forms coexists with illusion and even an adolescent naiveté. We must take these questions seriously, however. The reflections they stimulate can contribute as much to the greater flexibility and openness of the setting of religious life as to its necessary reaffirmation.

The answers depend on one's presuppositions, i.e., the understanding one has of religious life. According to the conception one holds of this life (as Gospel radicalism lived communal in celibacy, as Christian radicalism without any precise determination, or as an experience to be rediscovered) one's theoretical response and experimental search will be very different. In the latter two views, one can attempt anything not contrary to the gospel callings. It would still be necessary to have deep faith and solid common sense in order not to embark upon adventures which could ruin human lives.

The reader knows our idea of religious life and what we regard as the least satisfactory response to historical experience and Christian reflection. The reflections which follow take these as a point of departure.

1. Greater flexibility and openness.

The current tendency toward openness, receptivity, and the sharing of prayer, fraternity, the search for God and the service of men and women as well as the goods one possesses is certainly a positive value. The religious community thus ceases to be an isolated ghetto and comes to be what it should never have stopped being: a center of gospel life which receives from others as it gives to them.

Such a reception, suited of course to the concrete possibilities, should be available to all: men and women, individuals and groups, married and single people. Thus the community becomes truly a communion, a center of sharing and of dynamism. Those coming into contact with it will not be beneficiaries received paternalistically, but its active co-creators through their questions, experiences, and ideas. Beyond these spontaneous and sporadic contacts, we could even imagine some organized structures and co-responsibility.

In this regard, it appears particularly appropriate to revise the question of relations between the sexes. It is certain that the type of relations which prevailed until recently were marked by a systematic distrust and by regulations which seem anachronistic today (cloisters, parlors, etc.). While keeping a realistic attitude, it is clear that contacts must be made more simple, more open, that greater collaboration must be established on all levels, and that the other sex must no longer be regarded as a danger but as a fundamental complement on a human level as well as within religious life.

To be fair to the past, we should note that we are not the first to think of these things. All throughout history, religious groups have been centers radiating their influence through all states of life and attracting people from them. Oblates and tertiaries — to speak only of these forms which, even though they seem out of date today, are undergoing an astonishing renewal in some instances — responded in the past to the needs we mentioned: to be in communion with the centers of spiritual movements and share the same experience. We can and must conceive this communion in another way, in a more integrated fashion, but the simple desire for it is not absolutely new.

2. Maintaining an identity.

Must we then imagine a kind of open community where celibates, men and women, couples, and children all live together under the same roof, following the same discipline, sharing goods, table, and prayer? Generous as it may seem, such an idea appears to be more of a dream than a realistic project. Without a doubt we can envision a district or a village (for example, *l'Arche* in France or Reba Place outside of Chicago) where different groups put their goods in common or at least come to one another's aid, pray together, and share meals from time to time. But it is well when speaking of a community to make the necessary distinctions and no to confuse the styles. Are we speaking of a totally common life — cohabitation, community of goods, table, prayer, etc. — or of community in a wide sense — mutual aid, frequent contacts, common prayer? These are two realities which are ultimately profoundly different. The first case is a single cell, structured and similar in many ways to the family cell. The second, on the other hand, is a community constituted by uniting already-formed groups which keep their autonomy while associating with one another. To attempt to extend the scheme of community taken in its strict sense to this gathering of diverse groups which are more or less distinct in themselves is not only to fall into confusion, but to expose oneself to the worst mistakes. For, then one goes against the psycho-social laws which govern these groups. We will take these distinctions into account as we discuss both mixed communities (with celibates of both sexes) and the common life of celibates or couples.

If we are speaking of a communion of different communities, each possessing its own identity and autonomy but joined together on certain levels (the sharing of goods, work, prayer, etc.), then this would appear possible, although not without its problems, especially concerning the education of the children who cannot have their parents' choice imposed on them, no matter how close to the gospel that choice may be. Experience will show in the long run which values can be realized in this arrangement and what limits must be respected. The multiplication of experiences of this sort shows, at any rate, that a need exists thus to broaden the idea of community and to give a new face to that which is at the heart of the Church's mission. What a forceful sign it would be in the city of man for celibates of both sexes along with couples to create a real community where people know and love one another, share together, assemble to hear the word of God and celebrate the Eucharist! For, is not this the realization of our original dream and a sktech of what the new humanity will be like?

But when it is a question of a life lived totally in common, we are speaking of an altogether different situation. To put couples, children, and unmarried men and women under the same regime seems to us to be a dangerous utopia which ignores the laws of life in common. This is especially true regarding the mixed common life of celibates. Ideally, this would undoubtedly be the sign *par excellence* of our moving beyond genital sexuality and thereby a shape of the world to come. We can only hope, following the intuitions of Teilhard de Chardin,[31] that humanity will arrive at the day, even before the parousia, when there will be "neither man nor woman." Everything that happens in this direction today must be welcomed as progress. And yet when we see experiments of this kind here and there we must often ask whether they are not functioning under a serious ignorance of fundamental psychological realities. Is it truly possible for unmarried men and women to live together in a community where life is shared almost totally without slipping, through force of circumstance, into bonds which are oriented toward love and the formation of a couple? Are we not confronted with a profound law governing the relations between the sexes? And even if it were possible, it would still lack credibility from the outside. The sign would be too ambiguous, too fraught with suspicions and afterthoughts. In our civilization, the only totally mixed situation admissible is that of the couple and the family. And even here, certain limits are imposed in the case of young adults. It takes too much imagination and naiveté to believe that consecration to celibacy makes a single men and women brothers and sisters in the usual sense of the words. A celibate man must have as much distance and reserve toward women as a married man who intends to remain faithful to the woman he loves has toward other women. To believe and behave otherwise is to expose oneself to confusion and insurmountable difficulties.

3. Former religious.

One last point merits examination by reason of its currency — hopefully temporary. It concerns definitively committed religious who, for different reasons, have been released from their profession and, having left religious life, have opted for marriage. Even though there are few precise statistics on this point and we must

not generalize or exaggerate, in the last few years these departures have been more numerous than in the past. In certain orders
and certain countries, there is even a sort of hemorrhage. We can
be astonished at the ease with which dispensations from vows are
obtained today and think that the idea of commitment has thereby
been devalued. At least we cannot accuse the Church of being
legalistic and inhumane. Moreover, juridical practice follows situations of fact; if we are to deplore anything, it is more the personal decisions than the dispensations which ratify them.

Moreover, there are many reasons for these departures. There
were undeniably a certain number of religious who entered common life with essentially sociological motivations, mostly sub-
conscious: family pressure, the attraction of an image of a state
of life granting a place in society and conferring a respectable role,
the idea that one could give oneself to God only in religious life,
etc. Formation attempted to provide more solid motives based on
faith and free choice: theoretically, it succeeded. But with time,
the relaxation of institutional constraints, greater personal freedom, the general attitude of questioning and, occasionally, the
sudden departures of a number of people at once, many have
become aware of the error of their first decision. The possibility
of remaking the decision in its original meaning has not often
been grasped; many have preferred to make what they considered
a correction in their trajectory. To them the abandonment of a
religious option has seemed the reparation of an error.

Thus, the attitude toward those who thus leave has been modified in the direction of greater understanding. The links formed
in the years of common life have not been broken; friendships and
often the same spiritual necessities remain. Official Church associ-
ations have even been formed to help former religious make the
often difficult transition to concrete life.

But what should the relationship of the religious community be
toward those who, once totally involved in this life, have chosen
to leave it? We are discovering one aspect: respect and tolerance
for the freedom of others. On this level, there is still room for

progress. But must we go still further and consider that such a change can be a normal evolution, that a married brother can broaden the dimensions of the community, and that the community can allow within itself this passage from one state to the other?

It seems to us that if what we have said concerning life-long commitment is well founded. then to reason in this way would be to devalue this commitment and to destroy the reality of the community little by little. Even if in many cases the new decision does in fact rectify a previous error, the fact remains that it is an objective failure. One does not commit oneself for life after testing and reflection, one does not build together through the years, without the abandonment of this commitment creating some trauma on both sides. It constitutes the rupture of a contract understood to be lifelong. Relationships cannot be the same afterwards, in the interests of both the community and the one who has left. By trying to play both sides, the latter could lose his new vocation. As far as the community is concerned, it would finish by breaking up, if staying and leaving have the same value.

Chapter V

THE FUNDAMENTAL QUESTION: RELIGIOUS LIFE, FAITH, AND PRAYER

All that preceded, important as it may be, is only peripheral. The fundamental question remains to be raised: that of the link between religious life and Christian faith. What has been said constantly presupposes that one moves within the domain of faith, that the words "God," "Jesus Christ," and "gospel" have a vital significance, and that the realities toward which they point are at the root of religious and Christian commitment. We must now submit this presupposition to examination and critique, asking if and how it is the basis of religious life. In other words, we must examine the faith of religious: its crisis, its necessity, and its privileged expression, prayer. This might appear paradoxical and even shocking, since it might seem evident that religious life has no meaning outside faith and that the religious is, in himself, a witness to this faith. But as a matter of fact, the crisis surrounding religious life today — a part of the general crisis of the Church — reveals that the principle problem is precisely faith, which one can never suppose *a priori*.

I. SITUATION OF CRISIS

Religious life has always seemed, rightly or wrongly, a privileged manisfestation of the Church. Sociologically, the groups of priests and religious with the institutions they maintain and administer (churches, houses, apostolic works, etc.) seem to be the fundamental, if not unique, structure of that which is called the Church. On a level even closer to that of faith, religious and priests are considered specialists in religious affairs and "men of God." They are like the backbone or core of the Christian community. We recognize that such a view is tainted by clericalism and is faulty theologically; for, the community of the Church is present in all its members: laity, religious, and clerics. But it also expresses a reality: these men and women are linked, by their whole existence, to the reality of the Church, whether as leaders of Christian communities (priests) or as creators of a type of life which has no meaning outside faith (religious). Now this link is a sign of a link that is even more fundamental: that of faith. In fact, if we go to the heart of the matter, what gives the Church its existence is faith in the God of Jesus Christ and the mission it has to proclaim this faith as the foundation of all personal and collective existence. Thus, through this very identification of the Church with religious life one arrives at the ultimate question of faith.

To speak of faith in crisis today is almost to be banal; but it is also pertinent since true belief has never been something that remained unquestioned. It is true that there have been periods in the life of the Church when it was dangerous to believe: it could almost cost one his life. There were other times, on the contrary, when all called themselves believers and it was dangerous not to believe. But this is not to say that it was ever easier to believe; conformity can lead to a faith taken for granted, hindering essential questions and the possibility of a personal faith.

The present situation is somewhat peculiar; it varies according to the settings. Although there are Christians who even today must pay dearly for their faith (in certain countries where religious liberty is only a word), usually people are free in terms of their interior choice and their practice. The general phenomenon of freedom of thought as well as the disintegration of sociological structures favoring religious conformism makes the question of faith more and more personal. This often demands a certain nonconformity, an original and different option.

All the more so since the West, a civilization sprung from Judaeo-Christian roots, is today undergoing an identity crisis which brings the fundamental affirmations of faith into question. While searching for an ultimate meaning of life and displaying some interest in faith and religion, today's world does not accept their proposition uncritically. The very fact of belief — that is to say, of postulating and affirming for the person and the world a meaning which goes beyond men and transcends him — is submitted to a barrage of criticism. This criticism comes from different camps: the first, in the name of reason and science (neo-positivist currents: what exists and can be explained is that which is accessible through scientific investigation or logical rationalism); the second, in the name of modern psychology (the roots of man are fundamentally ambiguous and elusive, and religion and faith are projections of an unconscious search); the third, in the name of historical efficacy (Marxism: faith has only served as opium, it has not succeeded in transforming the condition of man and is therefore useless). Belief thus seems to be an irrational and purely subjective choice, charged with ambiguities and, moreover, useless. To proclaim that God is dead in such a condition is to affirm the end of an illusion and to call man to the realistic acceptance of his condition, without metaphysical reveries.

Although Christian faith is not directly linked to this approach — it is presented as based on a history — it is all the same reached by the criticism. While the God of Jesus Christ is not the God of philosophers and scholars, it is no less true that the rejection of the very idea of God and every meaning it can have on the level of intelligence would sunder faith from all rational roots and make it a purely subjective happening, an illusion. To be sure, once again, Christianity rests above all on faith in Jesus Christ who gives a meaning to man and to the world in opening them to an absolute future by the victory over death. But Jesus reduced to a simple human dimension is a basis for nothing. And if we confess him as an absolute meaning we refer ourselves —

whether we wish it or not — to what is called God. This is why there cannot be a Lord Christ (Jesus as an absolute and decisive historical event) if there is no living God.

But not only the idea and reality of God are called into question. The criticism assails the very foundations of Christianity: the historical reality of Jesus and the paschal faith of the Apostolic community. While no serious scholar can now deny the historical existence of Jesus and his death on a cross, certain exegetical approaches so reduce the historical substrata of the gospels that aside from his existence and death there is almost nothing of which we can be sure. There remains the faith of the primitive community, to be sure, to which all the documents witness (the letters of Paul, the gospels, etc.). But detached from history and interpreted by modern day hermeneutics, this faith appears as a simple self-understanding for which the message of Jesus was only an occasion. The resurrection of Jesus, touchstone of Christianity, is often reduced to mere evidence of the lasting influence of Jesus. Certainly, we are only speaking here of extreme positions usually held by critics who are unbelievers. But such ideas have wide currency, often through the oversimplified popularization wrongly attributed to this or that great theologian: Bultmann, Tillich, Bonhoeffer, etc.

Christian faith in God and Jesus Christ is exposed, then, to rational as well as pragmatic contestation. This contestation also affects Christians committed to religious life. For a long time the latter lived in very closed structures which protected — or gave the impression of protecting — faith. Religious life had very precise frameworks which demanded a constant effort and called for a motivation in faith, even if this motivation was often somewhat artifical. It was possible for structure and behavior to take the place of faith; committed to accomplishing their duty, religious had neither the thought nor the time to raise questions of faith. They were inserted into a system which itself referred to faith: this was presupposed. As long as the system lasted — and this is often still the case — it would have been incongruous to pose questions of faith since, in principal, everything was based on it.

But as we have already said, most of the protective structures are loosening up and disintegrating. Religious, like other Christians, are caught up in the general problematic situation; with all believers they face the same challenges and the same criticisms. Like priests — the other core of Christians strongly bound to a structure which supposes and requires faith — they are placed, if somewhat later than the others, before the same fundamental question today. In fact, it frequently happens that passing beyond the secondary questions (of the institution, the Church, religious life, meaning of ministry) one finds oneself confronted with the single question: what does it mean for me to believe? Am I a believer? Are these commitments I have made and which I try to live, the word which I proclaim, these religious motions I make — are they truly based on a personal faith? Is there a radical experience called faith behind this mask of words and poses? Confronted with such questions many hesitate. They are afraid that if they push too far they will fall into the void. Finding no real ground in the forms which sustained them (an illusion, perhaps), they dread recognizing and admitting that, as far as faith is concerned, they are only at the beginning. And the beginning is, perhaps, the confession that one's words and gestures were false and that one must begin to believe.

Thus the question of faith is the only true question. All other questions can be alibis, or escape from the essential. What a grace to be thus reduced to the only thing that counts!

II. BELIEF TODAY

Without attempting a profound treatment, it would be well to analyze at least briefly the question of faith in religious life. This analysis will include, first of all, a general reflection on faith, then some applications to the reality of religious life.

(a) *General reflection on faith.*

The religious, as we have seen, is firmly inserted in the structure of the Church, which is basically a structure of faith. He presents the world with an image of a confessing, committed Christian. He proclaims the faith of the community in his prayer, the privileged expression of Christian originality. The formulas are there: the Scriptural texts, symbols of faith, prayer forms coming from a distant tradition. If he has a certain theological culture — the general situation today — he knows the interpretations and meanings given to these formulas. These interpretations are diverse: some classical, some more recent and closer to his mentality, others clearly avant garde. But all try to shed light on the intelligible character of faith. We have here what can be called the objective datum of faith: a collection of concepts and images pointing toward an unspeakable reality — God, the resurrected Jesus — and explaining it in words and symbols. The religious lives in the midst of this universe, using it to manifest the meaning he gives his existence and which inspires his conduct.

But here a difficulty asserts itself. It happens that, becoming aware of this world of references, words, and symbols which serve as his environment and shape his life, he experiences it as something exterior, something unreal. It does not seem to grasp the depths of his existence; there is a gap between verbal affirmations and personal attitudes and experience. This God he confesses, whom he invokes, this Jesus become Lord and Christ, the new world inaugurated by the resurrection and in which the believer is supposed to participate, this absolute future open to man and woman and the world — what relation does any of this have with daily life? This life with its repetitive gestures, its practical considerations, its immediacy, and its narrow horizon — is it not tied to a reality which, although grandiose, effectively escapes not only all verification but all experience as well?

In short, the call of faith seems to address itself to a region of being which seems, for many, non-existent or at least atrophied. What is confessed as having definitive and total meaning apparently offers no orientation on the level of concrete life and the practical decisions of each day. The numerous questions raised by man throughout his interpersonal, professional, social, and political commitments do not seem to receive any direct response from his faith.

We think, in fact, that this impression rests on an objective fact. No, Christian faith does not hold the answers to questions which spring from immediate living: in the scope of the physical, material, relational, social, etc., man is left to himself and to the general experience acquired by humanity. Whoever waits for the gospel to give solutions or directives to these problems will find only deception, if he does not solicit from the text a meaning they do not have in themselves.

Christian revelation does not carry an answer, but only to the fundamental and unique question of man, the question of meaning. It is when man confronts his own proper mystery, when he experiences a vertigo in the strangeness of being-there, of being both aware and personal in the world, that this question is raised. Who am I, what is the meaning of my existence, is there a future for me, and what future? I ask these questions for myself, but also for every human like me, everyone to whom I am linked and with whom I exist. And not only for man but for the material world in which man has his roots and for which he is the point of consciousness.

Such a question — described here in theoretical and abstract terms — is existentially raised, we believe, by all men and women. Without it, man is not truly man: he is reduced to one dimension, he lacks the final depth, he is not open to the ultimate preoccupation. It is possible that the multitude of immediate preoccupations stifles this cry from the depths, or that man himself seeks through diversions to escape from a question which anguish before the unknown raises. But there is a moment, at least, in the life of every man and woman when this question raises itself. The well-understood Christian message, if it meets this search for meaning, certainly does not appear as an answer imposing itself necessarily and rationally, but

at least as an answer carrying meaning. Faith, then, will be
a cry of adherence to this meaning on the part of man.

The difficulty of which we speak and which consists of not
seeing the link between the search of man and the affirmations
of faith comes from a double source. On the one hand, it is
the search which has been relaxed or even completely abandoned: man is satisfied with small, immediate solutions and refuses, even unconsciously, to raise the ultimate question. The latter not being raised or avoided, one can understand that the
answer has no meaning and inserts itself into nothing, since
it is true that a given response, when there is no question, has
no meaning at all. On the other hand, even when man is engaged with the question of meaning, the answer of Christian
faith seems to have no relationship to it. The blame can be attributed, we think, not to the message but to its presentation
and its interpretation. It happens, in fact, that this message is
prescribed as something in itself, a collection of affirmations
undoubtedly logically related among themselves, but without
any real relation to man and his search for meaning. One confesses God and the resurrection of Christ in doctrinally exact
formulas, one affirms that this concerns man, but there is a miss-
ing link and contact is not established between the desire of
man and the coming of God. Now the message, while it is a
response to the question God planted in the heart of man in
making him as he is, is also apt to awaken the question even
when it is not raised. One has perhaps forgotten this aspect
of the message and, in overloading the answers, has neglected
to raise the questions — or rather, the fundamental question —
which this message presupposes.

It is when man situates himself at these depths that the message reaches him and seems meaningful on this most fundamental level of his existence. He understands then in a vital manner the objective reality of Jesus Christ and God who, existing
in themselves, are also for man, *"pro me."*

Jesus Christ is received as the herald of and witness to meaning. This meaning — that man is not a product of chance but someone wanted as a partner through love, that he is not made for death but for life, that the absolute future is open to every person and to the world itself — this meaning is proclaimed and fulfilled in Jesus Christ. Jesus teaches this, but also, victorious over death, realizes it first of all in himself, as the first element of the new world. Also, if Jesus proclaims a meaning, it is not a meaning exterior to himself: he, himself, *is* this meaning. He does not say that man can transcend himself by his own effort; Jesus presents himself as that transcendence in which we must integrate ourselves in order to have him so act in us as well. Jesus presents himself as the turning point of the world and the center of history because God is in him in a unique and absolute fashion as he is in no other man or woman. He is the Lord in whom the world finds meaning and support because between him and the mystery of God there exists a relationship and a union which is such that he is the Son of God.

Jesus as Christ and Lord refers us, then, to the indescribable mystery of God. For, when we confess what Jesus is and what he has done for us, we affirm that he has gone beyond the human condition and we have a glimpse of what it is that sustains him and us, what we call God: a word so overused and criticized today, and yet so often indispensable. But what is behind this word and the concepts for which it is a vehicle? The images and concepts, whatever their origin (Biblical, philosophical, etc.), are as necessary as they are inadequate. One must use them and continually pass beyond them, searching for the unique countenance they suggest. This countenance is primarily an absence: it is the solemn threshold man reaches when he has gone through everything, where he stops seized with reverence and awe. He holds himself at the gate of this mystery: he knows that beyond there is the All — or Nothing. He calls, cries out for the absence to transform itself into a Presence. Reaching this point, faith makes itself invocation and prayer; then it is truly and absolutely faith. For, prayer is essentially a call to this Presence. "We call prayer, in the pregnant sense of the term, that speech of man to God which, whatever else is asked, ultimately asks for the manifestation of the divine Presence, for this Presence's becoming dialogically perceivable. The single presupposition of a genuine state of prayer is thus the readiness of the whole man for this presence, simple turned-towardness, unreserved spontaneity."[32]

God, for whom faith gropes and whom it experiences as absence (to experience something as absent presupposes the certitude or at least the desire for its presence), is the ultimate foundation of meaning. Not as an impersonal postulate, an abstract limit, but as man's partner, a dynamic of love, a dialogic reality without which he would be only an indifferent principle. That is why any effort at reflection ceases upon reaching this point; rather than speaking of God, man begins to invoke God. He no longer needs to speak of faith, but to speak to God. For, as Buber writes, speaking of religion (identical to faith for him): "(It) is essentially the act of holding fast to God. And that does not mean holding fast to an image that one has made of God, nor even holding fast to the faith in God that one has conceived. It means holding fast to the existing God. The earth would not hold fast to its concept of the sun (if it had one) nor to its connection with it, but to the sun itself."[33]

The decision of faith is a personal and, consequently, solitary act. It is accomplished on the threshold of mystery, where no one else may proceed with us. And yet, Christian faith cannot be born nor fulfilled apart from a community. In fact, the message of salvation in Jesus Christ reaches us across a temporal continuity (in history) as well as a spatial one (believers who are everywhere). This message is proclaimed and received in the midst of a community. The resurrected Jesus and God in his inaccessible mystery are known and confessed primarily in the space called the Church. It is there — and no-where else — that the believer receives the answer to his search for meaning. One can accuse this community of many compromises, even betrayals, and yet where would we go and who could teach us God and Jesus Christ?

Thus, if our search for meaning leads us to Jesus and his absolute affirmation, Jesus sends us toward his Father through whom alone Jesus can have a unique meaning for us. But we can meet neither one nor the other aside from the company of our brothers and sisters: their assembly is the privileged place for us in time and space where faith is rooted and nourished.

(b) *Applications to the reality of religious life.*

Everything that has been said so far obviously applies to all Christian life, which exists only through faith. Without it, there can be practices, behavior, community structures, but no Christians.

Religious life as social structure and especially as personal commitment is deprived of all meaning in the absence of faith. In this regard, the situation of the lay Christian is different. Everything constituting his life (his family, professional, social, economic situation, etc.) is made of the normal structures of human existence. These are aspects of life found in all men and women. It is true that faith gives all of this a meaning and therefore a foundation and new light influencing this life. But at this level faith does not create new structures unique to itself. The only original structure it sets up will be the Christian community, particularly its function of proclamation of the faith and celebration of cult. Aside from this, almost everything in the life of the lay Christian is lived, at least exteriorly, in the same manner as the rest of men and women. If his faith disappears, his link to the community of faith and worship would be broken; but, in itself, everything else would remain the same. We do not deny that the absence of faith would create transformations of life in the long run, being thus emptied of meaning. But for most of itself, it does not need a reference to faith to exist.

Because of its relationship to faith, the situation of the religious is not the same. There are in fact structures in his communal and individual life directly dependent on faith. We are not speaking of prayer or cultural expression of faith: this structure is the same for both vocations. But as we have shown, that which constitutes the specific nature of religious life — i.e., celibacy lived in common with its consequences (community of goods, mutual obedience, etc.) — forms a particular structure. Even from a sociological point of view, we have here an original phenomenon; a new human reality is created first of all on the horizontal level. Men and women, renouncing the conjugal bond, have realized a community of life and sharing among themselves. This new reality (although it is not new in an absolute way: in fact, celibacy is also a human reality apart from religious motivation, as is community itself) is at once personal (it is the individual who opts and commits himself) and collective (a community is thus created). But although this is a reality of a human order — even if exceptional — its roots are sunk deep in the Christian faith. The decision giving birth to this type of life rests in fact on the promise of the Lord and on the surrender of oneself to his word. And, that such a decision be maintained and be creative of a permanent project, it must ceaselessly define its relationship to the Word which gave it birth. In a word, the fundamental structure of religious life is directly dependent on faith. If faith should weaken or die, this structure not only becomes meaningless but self-destructive, since no root motivation remains. There can be temporary exceptions; but, practically, religious life without faith would be a contradiction. In the euphoria of the beginnings — the discovery of human fraternity and individual liberty, of the material well-being a small group can realize — everything seems simple and beautiful. Any reference to faith can be glossed over and the common life can seem to have a meaning in itself; but can it really hold together in the face of problems and the routine of living? It is doubtful.

It is in this sense that the religious is in some way condemned to faith. If faith crumbles, one aspect — even human, horizontal — of his life ceases to have a meaning and thus a possibility of existence. If he wishes to continue, he is returned, by the very structure in which he lives, to the decision of faith. Religious life requires faith for its existence and, because of this, it continually appeals to faith. At the same time it manifests faith, not primarily through its language, but by its simple existence as a special type of life. There is truth, then, in the affirmation that religious life is a particularly striking confession of faith. And when we speak of faith, we are not merely making a Biblical reference to any particular text (that, for example, on which celibacy is based!), but a reference to the mystery of God and Jesus Christ such as we pointed out above. Thus, beginning with an incontestably original structure, albeit of a human order (a community based on celibacy), the religious is gradually pushed to the ultimate question: of the meaning life — his life — can find in faith.

But this leads to a certain number of consequences. One cannot commit onself to the project of religious life if one's faith is not solid enough to create and carry durable structures. Not long ago such a faith was too easily presupposed: it was believed that a Christian had faith from the moment he sought to join a community and what followed was merely to introduce him to the specific demands of religious life. Now it often happened, in fact, that his motivations, however strong, were linked to social and psychic considerations having little relationship to faith. Today it is increasingly clear that as the structures loosen up or even disappear the fundamental faith must be strong enough to give meaning to the commitment. If such is not the case, everything disintegrates very rapidly. Could those already committed who are confronted with the emptiness of their personal faith live for any length of time in a structure stripped of all meaning? And how can a man without faith choose a life having a meaning only in the eyes of faith?

In speaking thus, we do not pretend that one can measure the degree of faith of a believer. Even less, that anyone can boast of a faith which has achieved perfection. We are all beginners, hardly yet committed to the long adventure of search and discovery, absence and presence. Religious life, which demands faith from the start, is also a school of faith, the place where faith is unceasingly challenged to new growth. But, more than in the past, it is necessary for each one to examine the very roots of his religious decision. Is it based on faith? What faith? For a faith which is too delicate or even a simple wish to open oneself to a faith which might come does not constitute a sufficient basis for building a religious life. Certain ancient rules — of St. Francis of Assisi, for example — required in a time of doctrinal uncertainties that one assure oneself of the faith of a candidate. In a very different context today, these recommendations hold their value: to commit oneself to religious life, one must at least have begun to believe, and in these times this cannot be presupposed of anyone, not even of those who have already been committed for some time.

III. PRAYER, PROCLAMATION AND CELEBRATION OF FAITH

Faith seen from the human angle is the convergence of all existence — one's own, that of others, and that of the world itself — in a single point which gives coherence and orientation to it all. This unique point is Jesus of Nazareth, acknowledged and proclaimed as Lord and Christ. Once linked to this focus of meaning, man discovers himself, discovers God and is able to read the meaning of the world and of history. This attachment, this adherence to a personal reality who is the source of meaning gives a solidity and at the same time a kind of solemnity to existence. Faith thus comprises a permanent dynamism supporting life, influencing all its dimensions and orienting it in spite of obstacles toward the absolute future.

At the same point where this convergence occurs, faith is an encounter, for he who carries meaning is a living and personal being. To discover him, to glimpse him as the source and foundation of all reality is the primordial experience of faith.

So, faith and prayer merge; to encounter means to recognize the Other as partner, to address him as "Thou," to call upon him. To be before this Presence, to know it receives us, to perceive that it unfolds and gives itself to us, to become aware of the bonds linking us to it — here are words trying to express faith and prayer in their identity. This experience of faith/prayer underlies all Christian life: it alone prevents intellectual reflection on faith and its understanding from degenerating into ideology, and morality from becoming a non-transcendent humanism. In this sense, not only does faith require prayer, it is prayer.

The mystery of encounter takes place in the most personal and incommunicable depths of man. Encounter is not within his capacity nor a fruit of his efforts or techniques. It is pure gratuity, silence. It can grasp man in any situation, at any moment. However, there are moments which, while they do not produce encounter, widen the space within which it can take place. These are the moments of solitude, of distance from self and others, of descent into the depths, of listening silence. Without them, man is prey to the flux of the immediate and to diversions which keep him on the surface. The necessity of creating a space for faith, for the development of its awareness and its interior explanation, is the necessity of individual prayer. To be sure, seen from the viewpoint we are developing, faith/prayer is an act encompassing and undergirding life in all its dimensions. In itself, faith/prayer can coexist with all the activities of man, not only as a separate or simply parallel reality, but as the ultimate depth in which life is rooted. Nevertheless, it is a law of man that all permanent but diffuse dynamism needs to be recovered, refocused, and re-acknowledged. In order that the essential realities of existence — life, love, death, freedom — do not lose their meaning in the daily routine, man needs to awaken them from time to time, bringing them to awareness, living them intensely, giving them some expression. A loving couple or very close friends carry their love with them at all times like a melody continually playing at the heart of their everyday existence, banal as the day may be. But moments apart, moments of meeting, sharing, and gratuitous intimacy are necessary or else the sentiment is likely to fade. Individual prayer plays this role for the believer. All that sustains his faith — the Word of God, sacraments, meeting with others, events — must be gathered together, remembered, relived at certain special times, in the solitude and silence of the individual conscience.

But since faith is lived as a communal reality, it needs collective expressions as well. The most rich and total expressions as well. The most rich and total expression is the communal celebration of prayer. Here, through its content, one finds the whole Christian mystery expressed in its extraordinary variety, its historical and communal dimension. The Word of God transmitted through the Scriptures and the many responses to faith through the centuries are proclaimed, acknowledged, and confessed. The sacraments, when they are celebrated (in religious groups, this means Eucharist and penance almost exclusively), make the real intervention of God in the transformation of man and the world concrete through the symbolism of ritual. Thus, the celebration of prayer for the Christian community is the privileged expression of faith as the call of God and the response of man. It is the confession of faith in act. In it, in effect, the whole universe of historical revelation is gathered together and condensed. After the believer enters into it through his intelligence, his heart and his body affirms that he is a part of this universe, that he recognizes the meaning conferred on his existence by the coming of God in Jesus Christ. Through this rich language, vehicle of the old and the new, intellectual and symbolic at the same time, appealing to the personal decision as well as communal celebration, the community sings its confession of faith, its reason for living, its roots.

As for the form that prayer assumes: it is a celebration, a feast. It is not only speech of the rational and theoretical or practical and moral type, it is a language charged with images and reminiscences, a poetic language. There is more. This word constituting the heart of the celebration is not only spoken; it is sung and played, accompanied with postures and gestures, in a particular space, by a man expressing his wholeness through certain objects (clothing, things of beauty, etc.). Thus man desires to express the ultimate dimension of his existence in the most total language available, using the whole range of possible means of expression. The celebration of prayer is to the individual and communal experience of faith what the theatre, literature, poetry, music, and song are to the essential questions of man. With its proper language it expresses, on a register similar and close enough to these activities, the ultimate preoccupation of man and the response offered by faith in the God of Jesus Christ.

As confession and celebration of faith, prayer is then supremely proper to the Christian. Intellectual discourse, exchange between persons, individual reflection, concrete commitment are indispensable parts of faith, but still partial approaches and expressions. In prayer, an entry into faith and an all-encompassing expression are proposed. It is then the exterior activity most closely linked to the interior act of faith; it is the place where faith manifests itself, at least objectively, with the most intensity. So, without prayer (sacraments and cultural celebration) neither faith nor Christianity can exist. A Christian community, whatever else it may be, has its proper existence only here; and the measure of its prayer (quality, depth, frequency) is the measure of its faith.

For religious life, based as it is on faith, this is an absolute necessity, even on the sociological plane. It must build each day on faith and thus prayer, lest it dissolve into a vague humanism or disappear in a short time. It has done this more or less well throughout history, and not without fidelity. Today many religious environments face questioning not only on the style of prayer, but even on its necessity. Should we not live like other Christians — at the most with a Eucharist from time to time? We will return to this problem of frequency. As for the necessity of common prayer in a religious group, it seems to us as important for this group as the necessity of confessing and celebrating the faith is for all believers.

IV. FORMS OF PRAYER

The primary problem of prayer is one of faith, since prayer is nothing but a coming-to-awareness of the bond joining man to the God of Jesus Christ. When this bond is perceived, or at least when its absence is experienced as a lack, a desire, then faith, as well as prayer, is born. The forms which come to express and sustain this primarily interior experience are at once indispensable and relative. Indispensable for man since, as an interior being projecting himself into the world through his body and word, expression is a necessity of his nature; at the same time it expresses the depths of that nature, it creates it. They are relative, nevertheless, for on the one hand they are meaningless without the depth of faith, and on the other hand, they vary from age to age, among groups and according to cultural milieu. This relativity is nevertheless limited in Christianity by the necessary reference to the event which took place once and for all and of which we await the final fulfillment.

We must stop to insist somewhat on the problem of forms, arising from the current situation of prayer in the evolution of religious life.

Prayer, as we have seen, has always occupied a place in religious experience. Even when its requirement, which we believe to be a common demand on all, was practically and often theoretically diminished — "ordinary" Christians prayed less and less — religious maintained the practice of the early Church: they met many times a day for prayer. This has lasted practically until our day.

The style and framework of this prayer were "sacred." The texts used, the musical accompaniment, bodily gestures, vestments, the place reserved for prayer and built for this purpose, the furnishings — all recalled the particular, separate character of this activity called prayer. It is true that apart from certain exceptions — monasticism, in particular — the forms and often the structures had become sterile and degraded. They were often only a skeleton or corrupt vestige of what in other times were celebration and feast. In spite of everything, there was a power: the richness of the texts, their poetry, their quality, the variety of rites, all carried a hidden vitality. Liturgical renewal and reform has attempted to eliminate the deformed aspects, rejuvenating and even recreating them: new forms, still imperfect and open to evolution, have emerged.

And yet there is a crisis of prayer among religious today. A crisis of the depths which is that of faith itself and its manifestations, but also, secondarily, a crisis of forms. We think the two are linked: if the latter is more strongly felt, it is both a symptom and an alibi. Contesting the forms is easier, but in the long run this makes us forget that the problem is elsewhere. The problem is essentially not *how* we express ourselves, but *what* we want to express. If the forms seem empty, is it only because they do not touch the experience of faith which we live? Is it not, rather, that there is often no experience to express? The forms can revive or sustain faith, but we cannot expect them to take its place. Saying this, and granting its importance, let us nevertheless re-examine the question of forms.

The crisis of prayer is acutely felt in the new experiences we mentioned in the beginning of this volume. These small groups live in apartments where there is no place reserved for prayer and where work schedules often prevent regular times of meeting. The old forms and even those proposed as renewals, the texts with their style and centers of interest, the verbal images, the necessity of a certain solemnity, all often appear out-of-date or, in any case, unadapted to the situation. How can one celebrate the Eucharist around a kitchen table or in armchairs and couches? How can we sing or even recite the formulas with a group of three or four, especially when the language used, poetic and of a certain gravity, seems out of place in such a situation?

Confronted with these problems, two attitudes are possible. First, one can either minimize or simply suppress all rite and all expression, clinging to the verbal formulas of prayer and the Eucharist. But these texts, spoken or read (in the tone of voice that is used) quickly seem unreal, disproportionate; there is discord between what is being said and the insignificance of the voice saying it. In the second alternative, faced with this malaise, this gap between content and its concrete expression, one can reject the language used in liturgy and seek to create new forms and new rituals. The tendency would be toward simplification, reduction, the use of every-day language and the forms of ordinary life. One would pray as one talks: the same language, the same tone of voice; one would try to make the Eucharist resemble an ordinary meal, or going even further, to see the Eucharist in every meal. In order to bring prayer close to life, for it to be within life, one would want that there be little difference or separation between it and other activities so that the time would come when one would not want to create one more activity distinct from the others.

These attitudes, somewhat exaggerated in our description, are not purely imaginary; they exist in fact, among many groups where the question of prayer is raised and where few links to law or little social pressure are felt. It seems to us that they raise a question concerning the form of prayer, a question deserving of serious reflection.

We have said that prayer is a reality of faith; it is faith in its most intense action. On this level, it is an object of theological reflection, and this reflection was covered in the preceding pages. When it comes to a question of the form of this prayer — its verbal expression, its content, its particular style, the space it creates and in which it unfolds, its festive character, etc. — the question before us is above all anthropological. We must examine the register of human activity where prayer is situated, the laws it follows in its concrete expressions.

Now, looking at what we consider as prayer, both within and

without Christianity, we notice that it constitutes a particular activity. We want to say that it cannot be identified with this or that other activity of man. In fact, the life of men and women is made up of multiple activities, all distinct one from the other, all "apart" in some way. Sleeping is different from eating and working is not resting; reading or discussing, talking or playing, all are particular activities. On the simple plane of exterior expression, prayer is one among these activities, apart from them, different from each of them. Although prayer, in the meaning of contact with God, can coexist on the level of faith with all the activities of a person which it sustains without seeming to be a distinct reality — it is then secret, interior — once it is expressed visibly as a communal fact, it appears as a specific act. It seems to us that this is empirical evidence: prayer which is expressed exteriorly takes its place among the other human activities, with requirements and characteristics proper to it.

Each of the special types of human activity has its own structure and follows its own internal laws. A meal carries a certain style, and the more culture is introduced into it, the more it becomes a celebration regulated by rites. Writing or listening to poetry or music demands different attitudes and expressions of a person than would making small talk or carrying on a passionate discussion. A speech also follows laws, differing according to content or audience it is true, but always underlying whatever is said. And when we come to the realms of acts concerning a group, a community, the structures become more rich and the laws of expression more complex.

If we ask what genre prayer comes closest to, examining forms throughout history until today, we could say it is in the category of play, feast, and celebration like theatre or mass celebration. It is a kind of spectacle requiring the participation of everyone present, a total theatre where all express themselves following pre-established models. In fact, the language used is that of imagery and poetry, pregnant with symbolism. It runs the gamut from singing to solemn speech to entreaty. In so doing, through its multiplicity of expressions, it matches the greatest productions in the theatre. But there is more than language: a person also participates by means of his body, his postures, and his gestures. That which extends a person, gives him expression, is also of importance. Hence, vestments which signify a festival and complete and ennoble man, the place where the celebration takes place, the decor which creates an atmosphere (lights, flowers, pieces of art) — these are all linked to the heart of the activity as poetic expression. The question is raised: is there another level of expression where faith can be manifested in a better way? We do not think so, for this kind of expression is characterized precisely by its all-embracing character: all the dimensions of the person are being put into play and utilized. In prayer, the person situates himself before God in the totality and plenitude of his being for a festival.

If all this is convincing, it is not possible to reduce prayer, even in small groups, to an informal discussion group or a spontaneous improvisation, nor the Eucharist to a simple meal recalling the Last Supper. Such a reduction of language and rite leads little by little to rational discussion or sentimental small talk, ending with the pure and simple abandonment of prayer, since it has become degraded and contemptible. We can and must seek new forms, more simple and more adapted to the poverty of our language, our music, and our settings. The corner of a room, even if set off as a domestic chapel, is not the choir of an abbey, and a little table reserved for the Eucharist is not the stone altar of our old churches. It is equally certain that the poetic and musical richness of the word is often out of proportion for the small community proclaiming it. It is then necessary to create something more familiar and less solemn, even at the risk of fumbling and bungling. But recognizing always that there are limits one cannot transgress without falling into a dessicated rationalism or sentimentality. Moreover, recent experiences show[34] that where prayer is taken seriously there has been a movement from an almost total rejection of forms considered as sacred, to their gradual rediscovery. Singing, postures, a place set aside, vestments for prayer have all little by little re-emerged. For, while it is possible from time to time to celebrate a spontaneous and informal prayer without rite, any prayer intended to be regular needs not only interior fidelity but visible structures to carry it if it is to be maintained. If rite carries the danger of formalism, its total rejection degrades prayer to a merely human reality and leads toward its abandonment.

One point remains to be discussed: the frequency of common prayer in a religious community. Those who want or can still pray "seven times a day" are rare among religious. However, there are those who believe that prayer must be spontaneous, according to the inspiration of the moment; if there is to be a regularity, it should be very minimal: once a week, for example.

Now experience in the life of a group shows that spontaneity in this realm risks never becoming manifest: it is not certain that the whole group together ever spontaneously experiences the need to pray. A certain organization thus seems indispensable if prayer is to exist at all. As far as frequency is concerned, one daily meeting for prayer appears to be the necessary minimum; two or three moments (morning, noon, and night) is the ideal, note only to be hoped for, but to be faced as a possibility in most cases. All depends on the value accorded this central expression of faith. If one begins there, one can always make arrangements and organize one's life, no matter how chaotic and active, to allow time for this value. In any case, it is necessary to accord prayer the required time and to surround it with a climate of recollection and silence. It is undoubtedly better to have one period during the day, provided it is of sufficient length and calm rhythm, than to have three hasty and ill-conceived meetings. The introduction of long periods of silence into the common prayer will favor interior stillness and permit the combination of celebration and individual prayer.

As far as the celebration of the Eucharist is concerned, we should ask if its frequency need be daily, especially if it in fact takes the place of other forms of prayer. We ask this question because often, this is the solution adopted: the only gathering for prayer is the daily Eucharist. It seems to us that here we face the danger of devaluating the Eucharist and impoverishing prayer in general.

The Eucharist, certainly, is the summit of prayer and the central act of the Christian community. Without the Eucharist, the community could not exist: there it finds its roots and is regenerated. And yet, its too frequent use has its pitfalls. The most obvious comes from the very form of the Eucharist: its invariable character. Even if it is possible to introduce a certain variety into the Eucharistic prayer, the essential part always remains the repetition of the thanksgiving and the sacrifice of the Lord. Taking it up too often may engender monotony, inattention, and routine. The festive character, the "solemnitas" is lost little by little; for, what becomes ordinary is no longer festive nor solemn. And if the Eucharist takes the place of all other prayer, there will be a definite impoverishment: texts, forms, a certain flexible, more evangelizing approach are all abandoned. The Eucharist becomes a cure-all; every time one thinks of prayer one will celebrate it without realizing that one devaluates it, for *"assueta vilescunt."* A certain restraint, then, seems appropriate. It seems better to us to celebrate a weekly (Sunday) Eucharist with all possible dignity — obviously adapted to circumstances and occasionally under more simple forms one or more times during the week — than to seek an easy way out.

Whatever the case, prayer remains at the heart of religious life. To the very extent that this life is less and less distinguishable by its style, work, and commitments from every other type of life, the sign of prayer takes on importance as a proclamation of faith, as a manifestation of what carries and enlivens the Christian. Here, in fact is, the sign proper to the Christian (and religious) life as such. We think that the future of both hangs on fidelity to prayer. Hence, the crucial importance for both faith which is at the heart of prayer, and for the forms it must use (or even invent, perhaps) to find a better expression of it as a visible sign offered to all.

CONCLUSION

In the general questioning which is shaking the whole Church, what will happen to religious life in the next decades? Will it perhaps disappear? Under which forms will it subsist? Will these present-day currents which run through it and push it toward new searches be affirmed as the bearers of the future, or simply as passing whims? What will remain of what we see today and the reflections we have proposed? No one has a clear and definite answer to these questions.

We simply think that what lies at the heart of religious life — its desire for Christian radicalism, the sign of a community of love, the gospel possibility of celibacy — are facts which cannot disappear in the Church. As has been the case since the Apostles, there will always be Christians who commit themselves to this way; otherwise there will be no gospel, no Church. As long as this sign exists, there will also be a proclamation of Christian and human freedom.

In effect, such a type of life organized in community in the midst of the Church delivers it from the institutional rigidity which menaces it endlessly. It is a spontaneous surging, a manifestation of the freedom of the spirit: men and women rise up to show through their commitment where lies the c e n t r a l project of the gospel and the Church, its servant. The always-new and ever-reborn forms recall that one can never shut up everything inside an institution, that there is always a need for disturbance and alertness.

When they begin to live according to the gospel, Christians challenge the society in which they find themselves. In creating something new — a community of love and sharing where the individual is received and respected, where he is neither crushed by work nor alienated by a consumer society — they show by their existence the freedom that is possible in the midst of a highly technical society. They then accomplish a critical function in relation to Church and society, much more by affirmation —through creating something — than by a simple verbal contestation.

But this is an ideal, as we have said many times, which concerns all Christians. Religious try to live it for better or for worse, and it would be abusive to deduce from what has been written here any sort of triumphalism or self-praise. It is much more a question of a call, a demand, which is never the work of man but the fruit of the Spirit.

Francis of Assisi, in one of his genial intuitions, said that the true minister general of his fraternity was the Holy Spirit.[35] It is only the Spirit, source of all charisms, who can produce this life and this liberty today. He does and will do so utilizing human weakness, for in this way the power of God shines forth most strikingly.

NOTES

1. A. Favale, *Per una presenza viva dei religiosi nella Chiesa e nel mondo* (Elle di Ci, Turbin, Leumann, 1970, 1,020 pp.) contains an excellent bibliography for the postconciliar period (pp. 889-930); cf. also J. M. Beltran, *La vida religiosa y el Concilio Vaticano II, Orientacion Bibliagrafica, 1960-1968,* Verdad y Vida, 27, 1969, 496 pp.
2. *Celibacy and Community,* Chicago, Franciscan Herald Press,
3. "La vie religieuse au tournant." in *Nouvelle Revue theologique,* 101 (1969), pp. 834- 848.
4. See, among others, G. Thils, in *Ephermerides Theologicae Lovenienses,* 1967, no. 3-4; J. P. Torrell, *Revue Thomiste,* 1968, no. 3, pp. 491-492; P. Jacquemont, *Revue des Sciences philosophiques et theologiques,* 52 (1968), pp. 559, 575; P. Lippert, *Ordenskorrespondenz,* 11 (1970), pp. 109-110.
5. *La Documentation catholique,* 51 (1968), no. 1537, pp. 348-349; no. 1551, p. 1097.
6. *Acta Ordinis Fratrum Minorum,* 87 (1968), f. 1-2, p. 111; 88 (1969), f. 4, p. 200.
7. *Leur Aggiornamento,* Lyon, Ed. du Chalet, 1970, pp. 125-126; *Annuario Pontificio,* 1970, Citta del Vaticano, p. 882.
8. *La Documentation catholique,* 52 (1970), no. 1563, p. 495.
9. *Acta Ordinis Fratrum Minorum,* 87 (1968), f. 1-2, p. 126.

10. These figures and those which follow are from *Annuario Pontificio,* 1970.
11. On secular Institutes, see the recent book by E. Mazzoli, *Gli instituti secolari nella chiesa,* Ed. Ancora, Milan, 1970.
12. *Leur Aggiornamento,* cited in note 7, presents a general view of the work of capitulars in the different male orders.
13. Cf. *La Documentation catholique,* 51 (1969), no. 1551, p. 1047.
14. Such a view is expressed, for example, by Jan Ernst in "Ordensleben in einer weltlichen Welt," in *Christ in der Gegenwart,* 2 Nov. 1969, pp. 349, 350.
15. *Information catholiques,* no. 341-342, August 1969, p. 15; no. 367, 1 Sept. 1970, pp. 4-6.
16. The most systematic exposition of this perspective is given by Alkuin Heising, "Benediktinisches Mönchtum und Biblische Botschaft," in *Liturgie und Mönchtum,* Laacher Hefte, Heft 43, 1968, pp. 13-19.
17. At the moment, one of the better approaches seems to be by E. Cornelis, "Phenomene universal de la vie religieuse," in *Lumiere et Vie,* no. 96, Jan.-Feb. 1970, pp. 4-24.
18. On evangelical radicalism as a distinctive mark of religious life, see the sound article by J. M. R. Tillard, "Le fondement evangelique de la vie religieuse," in *Nouvelle Revue theologique,* 101 (1969), pp. 916-955. What follows shows, at the same time, our fundamental accord and the questions which must still be asked, in my opinion.
19. For the texts of the rules of Basil, Augustine, Benedict, and Ignatius, we have used the German collection by H. Urs von Balthasar, *Die grossen Ordenregeln,* Benziger, 1961. For St. Basil, see *Les Regles Monastiques* (trans. Leon Lebe), Ed. du Maredsous, 1969.
20. The article by A. Durand, "Recherche sur le sens de la vie religieuse," in *Lumiere et Vie,* no. 96, Jan.-Feb. 1970, pp. 54-90, puts it in the same perspective.
21. A. G. Martimort, *L'Eglise en Priere,* Desclee, 1961, pp. 794-795.
22. M. M. van Molle, "Vie commune et obeissance d'apres les Institutions Premieres de Pachome et Basile," in *Supplement,* no. 93, May 1970, pp. 196-225.
23. For the following analyses, cf. H. Urs von Balthasar, *op. cit.*
24. Cf. *Celibat et Sexualite,* colloquium of the Catholic Center of French Physicians, Ed. du Seuill, Paris, 1970, pp. 13-14.
25. *Adv. Haer.,* IV, 38, 4 ("Sources chretiennes," no. 100, Ed. du Cerf, 1965, p. 959).
26. J. Dupont, *Mariage et Divorce dans l'evangile,* Desclee De Brouwer, 1959, especially pp. 166-174; Q. Quesnell, "Made themselves eunuchs for the Kingdom of Heaven," in *Catholic Biblical Quarterly,* 30 (1968), pp. 335-358.
27. The most interesting studies on this aspect of celibacy seem to us to be, M. Oraison, *Le celibat,* du Centurion, 1966; Y. Pentener van Vlissingen, *Approches psycholgiques du celibat,* Presses de Taize, 1969; *Celibat*

et Sexualite, cited in note 24; Massart, "Le sens humain de celibat," in *Lettre aux communautes de la Mission de France,* March-April 1970, pp. 79 ff.

28. H. Urs von Balthasar, *op. cit.,* p. 41. On the subject of commitment, especially its historical and philosophical aspects, interesting comments can be found in the volume published after the editing of this text: *Engagement et Fidelite* (Coll. *Problemes de Vie religieuse),* Ed. du Cerf, 1970.

29. G. Gusdorf, *La Parole,* PUF, p. 116.

30. A. Veilleux, "Evoluzione della vita religiosa nel suo contesto storico-spirituale," in A. Faavle, *op. cit.,* note 1, pp. 23, 24.

31. *Energie humaine,* Oeuvres 6, Ed. du Seuil, 1962, p. 96.

32. Martin Buber, *Eclipse of God,* Harper and Row, New York, 1957, p. 126.

33. *Op. cit.,* p. 123.

34. P. Hamon, "Habiter le provisoire," in *Lumiere et Vie,* no. 94, July-Oct. 1969, pp. 21-26.

35. Thomas de Celano, *Vita II,* no. 193; cf. English translation by P. Hermann in *St. Francis of Assisi, Writings and Early Biographies,* Franciscan Herald Press, Chicago, Ill., 1973.